INTIMACY

by Beverly Angel

How To Become A Best Friend
& A Lover Of God

Unless otherwise stated, all scripture quotations are taken from the King James Version of the Bible.

ISBN 978-0-955 8116-9-2

Copyright 2011 by Beverly Angel
Published by Spirit Library Publications

Printed in the United Kingdom of Great Britain. All rights reserved under International Copyright law. Contents and or cover may not be reproduced in whole or in part in any form without the express written consent of the publisher.

Chapter One

Romancing the Heart of God

Some time ago my husband and I were on holiday in a certain country, deep in a tropical rain forest. The hotel was so well hidden it is known as the 'invisible lodge', big on posh cabin charm and modern art, heated marble from floor to wall, floor to ceiling windows overlooking plush green nature and the whitest sand beach just meters away from the Hotel's well manicured turf where we were sitting. It was by far the best we had ever seen. As we sat in front of our living room looking at this wonder that God created, we had a visitation from the Lord and we heard God's voice instructing us to teach his people 'intimacy' – how to be deeper lovers of God and how to be His best friends!

As the voice of the Lord continued, He directed our eyes to couples sitting by the sea front, some married, some in adulterous affairs and yes, some unmarried. Some were walking hand in hand, some were in each other's arms, and others were seated in their partners' laps while some feasted on oysters and some of the country's finest delicacies in front of a roaring fire. "All these are looking for intimacy," the Lord said. "They want a love and a lover who will not let go. They search this love in all these things yet I am the only one who can offer that."

This was something we thought we already knew but it came to us in a different way that day. It had more force and urgency to it than what we had in our spirits. It carried a forceful boom to it especially when God uttered the words that will make the carnal man mad "teach my people intimacy and build me a people that can romance My heart." Remember what the bible says about the carnal man:

1 Corinthians 2 vs.14
The carnal man cannot understand the things of the spirit Neither can he know them for they are spiritually discerned.

God wants people that can romance His heart. Believers that are so knit together with Him that it's not possible to separate them from God no matter what happens. Apostle Paul knew this and he uttered,
Romans 8 vs. 38,39
For I am convinced that neither death nor life, neither angels nor demons, neither the present nor the future, nor any powers, neither height nor depth, nor anything else in all creation, will be able to separate us from the love of God that is in Christ Jesus our Lord.

This is the level of life the believer will get to after getting equipped with the power of intimacy. It opened our eyes further and ushered us into higher levels of commitment and made us experience open heavens in our ministry and in all other affairs of life.

Right there and then, in that tropical forest hotel, the Lord Jesus filled us with the Spirit of wisdom concerning intimacy that can usher a man or a woman into a level where we can negotiate with God. A level of intimacy where believers can be so intimate with God that there will be an intermingling of God and His people to such an extent that the supernatural becomes natural for those that dare to be INTIMATE with Him.

Best friends of God...

When it comes to how to become a best friend of God, opinions here are like belly buttons – everyone has one. Many talk what they think instead of what the Lord has spoken regarding that issue. I am here by the Spirit of God to detail what the Lord told me about intimacy and not what opinions I might have. I shall be delving into the topic on how one gains an intimate friendship with God later on in the book. We are created for intimacy with the creator. We are created for a love affair with the one who made us and He is waiting for us to get to that level of love affair and friendship with Him where we have access into His secrets because we are dear lovers.

God loves His people and He is more willing to fall even deeper in love with them than they are willing to be in a love affair with Him.

You Are Created For INTIMACY

You see we are created to be close to God. We are made for the purpose of being in a deep relationship with the creator. We are made for intimacy.

A long time ago, Blaise Pascal, after years of studying Mathematics observed that there is a "God shaped vacuum" inside each and every one of us. He noticed that there was, is and always will be an empty place that only God can fill. In a nutshell Pascal realized, though a mathematician himself, that we are made for a close relationship with God. He got the truth that we are created for an intimate relationship with our creator.

Many feel there is something wrong with their relationship with God because they just lack one important thing in their walk with the Lord. That thing is romance. An ability to understand how to romance the heart of God gives one the ability to love and never to be moved and also gives one the keys for intimacy.

God is not a 'sugar daddy'

There is a culture in many Christians to treat God as a sugar daddy. We want what we want from Him and that's all that matters. When we praise Him it is so we can get something. Oh! What a mess. We have for too long gotten it all wrong. God yearns for affection and relationship. He wants us as a lover and groans for a relationship not built on us just taking and asking.

Intimacy

God yearns for romance, which is not carnal but spiritual. This is the heart of God for those He calls His children. We were created for intimacy and therefore we need to quit the attitude of treating God as a sugar daddy or an errand boy. That why He answers prayer not because we are praying but…

Psalm 66 vs.20
Blessed be God, who has not turned away my prayer, nor his loving kindness from me.

His love is the reason He helps us and that ought to set us straight if we think He answers prayer just because we have prayed. No, He is a God who is loving, kind and merciful.

Can one really romance the heart of God?

Romancing the heart of God is what He told me is possible. I have been there; I have seen it's possible. You know many times *a person with experience is never at the mercy of someone with a mere argument*. God has used me in extraordinary miracles and I am used in the prophetic in a mighty way that I can only give glory to God. I have experienced great signs, miracles and wonders in my ministry based upon intimacy with God. I have seen a lot of things in the spirit realm, secrets of future events based upon the secret to romancing God's heart that He gave me to teach His people who would listen.

Intimacy

Romancing the heart of God made it possible for me and the Lord to be closely knit together that which is His, became mine, so He tells me things. It's because romancing His heart made me gain access into His secrets. Do you see that? Romancing the heart of God is the greatest thing that we can do as believers.

In the Old Testament was a man who knew intimacy through obedience and great sacrifice that the Lord called him a friend. God loved this man to the extent that he could negotiate with Him. Abraham is the man and many think they know him but let me give you light on how he romanced the heart of God at a certain time. We shall take another look at Abraham in a later chapter but I just need to outline the type of intimacy and relationship this book is all about.

God was in a close relationship with Abraham that He saw no reason to hide His secrets from him. Why? Abraham though he received grace to be what he was, he had a secret, he understood intimacy. He knew how to get close to God. He knew how to romance God's heart. Remember before God said, 'Shall I hide from Abraham what I am about to do?' Abraham had done something for the Lord.

Notice what God did with Abraham;

Genesis 18 vs. 1-5
"...So he lifted his eyes and looked and behold three men were standing by him. When he saw them he ran from the tent door to meet them and bowed himself to the ground

and said, "My Lord if I have now found favor in your sight, do not pass on by your servant. Please let a little water be brought and wash your feet and rest yourselves under the tree. And I will bring a morsel of bread, that you may refresh your hearts after that you may pass by in as much as you have come to your servant." And they said, "Do as you have said."

Abraham had a heart for God that though he understood God to be a Spirit, he still begged Him to stay for lunch and he cooked the best meal that day because God had visited.

In verse 16 it says,

"... And the Lord said these words; `Shall I hide from Abraham what I am about to do?"

God and Abraham walked together so close, so intimate and so much in love with each other that God could say of Abraham;

Shall I hide from him what I want to do?

God was saying that He was doing something that in a sense did not relate to Abraham except for Lot but because this man was a man after God's heart, God wanted to share His plans with him. He felt compelled by love to share His secrets with Abraham. God wanted to share with a human being His intentions. And if that was not strange enough, stranger still was the fact that Abraham wanted to even negotiate with God about His plan to destroy a city.

Intimacy

In verse 20 of the same chapter,

"... But Abraham still stood before the Lord. And Abraham came near and said, " Would you also destroy the righteous with the wicked? Suppose there are fifty righteous within the city, would you also destroy the place and not spare it for the fifty righteous that were in it? Far be it from you to do such a thing." The Lord said, `If I find in Sodom fifty righteous within the city then I will spare the place for their sake"

Abraham was talking to God; he was not talking from a position of pride. Neither was he talking from a position of self-confidence but in a position of one the Lord had called a friend. Not as equals but as one who knew the Lord to be His king, Lord, boss and friend as declared by God himself. He still feared God and revered Him but he had a relationship with him. That's a very deep realm that he had moved with God. Abraham's statement here showed he was not approaching God saying, "I can come to God now freely." No, he was also aware that God was the One who is all-powerful. And there is an awesome fear of God that he was experiencing.

In verse27,

"Indeed now I who am but dust and ashes have taken it upon myself to speak to the Lord. Suppose there were five less than the 50, would you destroy it?"

Then he reduced it again and brings it to 40. Remember this is negotiation talk with the Alpha and Omega.

How many people could talk with God in that way? Here he started with 50. And he got God to agree on the 50 first and for the final time in verse 32, he says, "Lord, don't be angry if there were 10." God said, "I won't destroy it for lack of 10." The fact is from 50 he reduced it to 10.

Now most of the misunderstanding we have on romancing the heart of God is based upon many wrong teachings on the love of God, Agape and Philleo. This teaching has caused most Christians great hindrances. In our attempt to find things we can exclusively attribute to the devil or to the Lord we murdered the Greek language and acted like we know it by translating other words to mean something whilst we got others to mean something different. The church fed on the lies and everyone says they understand that God only has agape and does not have a part where he can be a lover of friend yet being lovers and best friends of God is what we were created to do. If a man in the Old Testament (which is a shadow of the New) could be called a friend of God and Israel a lover of God then we are to be lovers as well and better still, good friends.

The Lord Jesus Christ said,

Matthew 22 vs. 37
Love the Lord your God with all your heart and with all your Soul and with all your mind.

After saying that he uttered words many have not yet taken into their heart. He said

"...**this is the greatest command**..."
Verse 38

Now that word "love" is agape which means to love in a social or moral sense.

Many believers have been taught wrong. They think God only has agape. This is ignorance gone on rampage. God also allows philleo toward Him which in the strongest concordance itself is 'to kiss as a matter of tenderness and chiefly connected to the heart more than to the head'. Philleo means to have affection for, to be a friend to.

Apostle Paul gives us light when he says,

1 Corinthians 16:22
If anyone does not love the Lord, he is to be accused to be found of an entity or object.

The scripture says if you lack philleo you shall be as cursed. The word accused is a strong word "anathema" which means to be banned, excommunicated and to utterly be cursed all because one lacks philleo towards the Lord. People have been told all you need is agape and that no believer has philleo towards the Lord. What these ignorant people have done is a crime of the highest degree because the lie is so silly since its based on ignorance for language still exists today and anyone with an inch of brain capacity can research for themselves and see the open lie. God is agape and this is where we find the scripture,

1 John 4 vs. 8
He that loveth not knoweth not God; for God is love.
God is love and out of His agape there is philleo. God has affection toward us. Within agape there is philleo. So to teach people that God has only the agape kind of love is wrong.

Lets see what John says under the inspiration of the spirit,

John 16 v 27 says
For the Father Himself loveth you, because ye have loved Me, and have believed that I came out from God.

The word 'love' there is philleo. This means affection. This shows that even God possesses philleo towards his children.

God even says,

Matthew 10 vs. 37
"…he that philleo (loves) his father and mother more than me is
   not worthy of me. Anyone who philleo his son or daughter more
than me is not worthy of me"
In John 5 vs. 20 we see the Lord showing philleo love to the son,

"… For the father loves (philleo) the son and shows him all he loves…"

When it came to Lazarus the word says

"...the one you philleo is sick."
John 11 vs. 3

You see God has agape love, which added to this philleo results in His grace and mercy to provide salvation for mankind through His son Jesus. This is a bond that grants the ground for intimacy. God has agape and He also has philleo. The church has been told too many lies that feelings do not matter when it comes to our relationship with God. That is a half-truth. Feelings are tied in philleo and can be used for good and for bad.

See, feelings are not right when they are focused on the lusts of the world but if the word says "love your God with all your heart (spirit), with all your soul and all your mind", then I know this is something that requires all of me including my feelings.

Titus 3 v 4-5 proves it,
But after that the kindness and *love* (philleo) of God our Savior toward man appeared, not by works of Righteousness which we have done, but according to His mercy He saved us, by the washing of regeneration and renewing of the Holy Ghost"

John 3 vs. 16
For God so *loved* (agape) the world that He gave His only begotten Son that whosoever believeth in Him should not perish, But have everlasting life.

We have a mandate to know the differences of the love spoken of in these scriptures. God has agape and He also has philleo. Intimacy calls for everything you have. Romancing the heart of God is chief over everything. The art of romancing God's heart gets one into the very presence of God way beyond the veil.
Philleo is the love of things we have understanding of.

When most 'normal' Christians hear the words 'romancing the heart of God' they cringe at the statement simply because they have a carnal inclination to the words. The word 'romance' to most people means something too 'fleshly' and never something Godly. Romancing the heart of God is not about the flesh. It is about the spirit realizing a need to connect with God in a special way that creates a deeper walk. It is something that gets God to be more than a creator but a lover and a dear friend.

Intimacy comes by learning the art of 'romancing' the heart of God. Getting so close to His heart that one can really feel the 'heartbeat' of God. Drawing so near that, you can touch and feel the 'pulse' of God. You begin to understand Him by how He talks – every 'breath' as it were. Romancing the heart of God is like putting one's finger on the pulse of God and responding to every beat of His heart accordingly. Feeling His hurts, seeing His anger and knowing His likes and dislikes. It is getting behind the veil and seeing Him for who He really is.

This is easy to do but difficult to understand if you have a religious spirit or demon to put it plainly. The sensing of romance can overwhelm those that say they already know. You see it is difficult to fill a cup that is already full. Some will claim they already know how to get close to the Lord and draw nearer to His presence yet they would be mistaken. No wonder the word says it this way:

Matthew 6: 23
"...If the light that is in you be darkness you are in great Darkness!"

Don't claim you know when you don't know.

I have moved into these realms that is why the Lord awakened me to teach His people on how real intimacy can be achieved. God is more willing to be intimate with His creation more than the creation is willing. He is more willing to go deeper with us. He told me He wants us to get to a level in Him where there are no hidden things between Him and us.

This is what Apostle Paul got to once when he said the words,

1 Corinthians 2 vs. 10
"...but God has revealed these secrets to us by His Spirit..."

Apostle Paul was now in a position of knowing secrets because he had started 'romancing' the heart of God. He could now get the secrets hidden from ages past because 'romancing' the heart of God created intimacy. It gave him access into the vaults of heaven. As long as he was spiritually intimate with his creator there was no withholding information. There were principles that this Apostle had gotten to which created a wave in his spirit that intermingled with God's Spirit that there was nothing he could not have asked for of the Lord and not be granted it.

The Revelation...

This book is meant to create in you a deeper walk with the Lord. Intimacy that produces a kind of jittery excited love you feel that makes you nervous in the right sense. It makes your palms sweat, your mouth goes dry, your heart races with excitement, butterflies in your stomach and even words stumble clumsily out of your mouth for the Lord. This is not sexual love like carnal people would want to think. This goes way beyond sexual love. It goes beyond the physical love that people get so caught up with. It is in its own grade and dimension.

Romancing the heart of God creates intimacy between the creator and the created that is God and yourself.

Imagine that true lover...

Imagine that true love. Imagine the one you truly love. The connection I am talking about is not in the sexual sense. True lovers are friend's not just partners in the flesh. True lovers love to be together, they love to share, and they love to know what the other is thinking. True lovers do not hurt each other. They seek to understand and not just to be understood. True lovers are always together. They only see each other and only adore each other. Imagine that picture. Imagine it is you and the one you truly love. Just imagine that lover, never letting go and never letting loose. Imagine gazing into each other's eyes for eternity and realizing you never want it to end. Imagine that true lover as God.

That is exactly what God can be to you if you dare get the understanding of 'INTIMACY'.

Chapter Two

Becoming a friend of God

Some friends are like televisions. Some are like "Pay per view" television, they are always asking for money. Others are like the News, with tales to tell everyday and many not benefiting you at all. Some friends are like the advert channel, always changing and many are like that one station with the foreign language: you don't understand a lot of what they say but you listen and watch anyway.

The Lord Jesus on the other hand is a dear friend with a love you don't want to let go. The old singer called Him the fairest of ten thousand. He is a friend indeed. In fact He calls us friends Himself and not slaves. In fact He is more willing to be in a friendship with us more than we are willing to be friends with Him!

John 15 vs.15 (NLT)
I no longer call you SLAVES because a master does not Confide (tell His secrets) to His SLAVES. Now I call you friends.

Abraham knew the Lord to be a friend to the extent that even the Lord before He destroyed Sodom and Gomorrah passed by Abraham's house and uttered something that is mind boggling,

Genesis 18 vs. 17
How can we hide from Abraham what I am about to do?

God Himself valued His friendship with His creature called Abraham that He felt it difficult and even impossible to destroy a town, which Abraham wasn't even a citizen of without first telling Abraham.

Becoming a friend of God is not just a statement. There is more to it. It is like holding the pulse of God and knowing the heart of God at every moment. It is hating what He hates and loving what He loves. It is also about sacrifice. It is about willingness to let go and let God. Becoming a friend of God is to realize that only God matters. When this happens God begins to control things way before they come your way. David had the first hand experience. Look at this:

Isaiah 37 vs. 35
"For I will defend this city to save it for my own sake and for my servant David's sake…"

Did you see that? David went to bed during a battle, expecting to fight the next day but God being a friend of David stood up from His throne and killed the other army because of David. David only woke up to find the opposing army dead. God had killed them all.

God destroyed the enemies of His friend for two reasons, for His own sake and for David's sake. That alone is a revelation for true friendship. True friendship does not concentrate on one's own needs but looks and wills to solve the problem of the friend. No wonder the word says,

John 15 vs. 13
Greater love hath no man than this, that a man should lay down his life for his friends.

Friendship is an ability to give yourself away for the benefit of the relationship. If a believer wants to get to a deeper walk with God they ought to surrender all for the sake of the relationship. You give away the "I" for "we". A deeper walk with the Lord means one ought to cast away the spirit that says "I" and adopts "we". Sacrifice is the heart of the friend. There is a lot that God will do for His friends. Friends of God are different from people of God. Friends are told everything. See there are disciples then there are the multitudes. The Lord spent time with His disciples and told the multitudes things for a specific time yet stayed with the disciples whom He called friends.

Understanding the friend we have in Him

In order for us to become friends of God, we need to first understand His nature and person. The word of God speaks of two men who walked with God to the extent that they defied tradition and interacted with God as friends. They spoke and planned with God in a way that inspires many believers today.

The first man I have already mentioned earlier and this is Abraham; let's dig a little deeper and see what insight we have about his relationship with God;

Genesis 18 vs. 17
`Shall I hide from Abraham what I am doing?'

Did you see that? God and Abraham were so intimate that God could say of Abraham,

"Shall I hide from him what I want to do?"

In other words what God was saying was he wanted to share His plans with someone. His closeness and friendship with Abraham was so deep that He had to share His intentions with him first before carrying them out. The same is true right now if you take time to grow intimate with Him. In the book of Amos 3 vs. 7 God says,

"For God does nothing without telling His Servants the prophets."
Amos 3 vs. 7

He is the same God. He never changed from the days of Abraham. He wants us to have an intimate relationship with Him. He wants us to be in love with Him and to be loved by Him.

As if it is not surprising for God to consult Abraham first, even more baffling was the fact that Abraham could negotiate and converse with God about His plan.

Genesis 18 vs. 18
Since Abraham shall surely become a great and mighty nation. And all the nations of the earth shall be blessed in him. *For I have known him* **in order that he may command his children and his household after him that they keep the way of the Lord to do righteousness and justice that the Lord may bring to Abraham what He has spoken to him...**

God and Abraham were well acquainted. Someone once said that Abraham spoke to God from a position of pride and self-confidence but it certainly was not. Even though the whole conversation was a negotiation between God and Abraham, it was more of a plea or request on Abraham's part. He was entreating God and God was listening. This level of intimacy is very deep and believe it or not it is the very level God wants us to reach. It is not just for a chosen few. Your goal should be to become such close friends and lovers that no one could ever come between you. The word of God says God is love, which makes Him a lover. We are also lovers because we are just like Him.

We should be so close that we can negotiate and 'reason together' as stated in the book of Isaiah.

Come now, and let us reason together, saith the Lord Isaiah 1 vs. 18

The Lord God Almighty, our saviour is saying He desires a relationship with us that gets us to a level where we 'reason' with Him. Verse 27 of Genesis 18 tells us this,

"Indeed now I who am but dust and ashes have taken it upon myself to speak to the Lord. Suppose there were five less than the 50, would you destroy it? And God said, `If I find there 45 I will not destroy it."

This scripture proves the fact that Abraham had the utmost respect for God and his negotiation was not based on foolish pride. By first recognising that without God you are indeed nothing, you automatically allow Him room to come into your life and make you somebody. You have to learn to humble yourself and God will do the lifting up. He knew that God was the One who is all-powerful. See how the negotiation carried on,

"Lord, don't be angry if there were 10." God said, "I won't destroy it for lack of 10."

See God reduced the figure from 50 all the way down to ten. What a mighty God we serve! This level of intimacy is gained through time spent and dedicated to the one you love. It does not just start off on this level. The bible says

1 John 4 vs.19
"We love because He first loved us"

Before we cared much for Him or paid much attention to His word, He already loved us and that is the reason why we love. It is our nature. To move into deeper realms of intimacy we need to hate what He hates and love what He loves. It is also about sacrifice. It is about willingness to let go and let God. Becoming a friend of God is to realize that only God matters.

Giving alongside intimacy

Genesis 18 vs. 2-5
"My Lord if I have now found favour in your sight do not pass on by your servant. Please let a little water be brought and wash your feet and rest yourselves under the tree. And I will bring a morsel of bread, that you may refresh your hearts after that you may pass by in as much as you have come to your servant..."

I want you to notice that the first thing that Abraham did when he caught the revelation that the Lord had visited him, he gave. I call it a revelation because the bible says in verse one, "**...the Lord appeared to him....**" Yet what Abraham saw were three ordinary looking men approaching his tent. Upon perceiving that this was more than met the eye, he immediately rushed and knelt before the men and said "**...my Lord if I have now found favour in your sight...**". See that? He didn't say, "My Lord(s) or gentlemen let me introduce myself" NO! The man was fully loaded with revelation and deep intimacy with God that his spirit immediately knew its lover was on the scene. That is intimacy.

Abraham was so well acquainted with his friend, loved one and Father God that no disguise would work! He knew it in his spirit that these were no ordinary men coming for an afternoon chat about chariot races – it was Papa God Himself! Now knowing this, he immediately endeavoured to give something. Here lies an important key to intimacy. When you love God you give. You give because you are a lover by nature.

My husband and I love to give. We enjoy giving as much as we enjoy breathing. It is our nature, its part of us. Take away our giving nature and we are as good as dead – that's how important it is to us. Any opportunity we find to give we jump at it without a moments hesitation. We have sown in times of lack and in times of plenty and God is faithful all the same.

There was a time when giving was not my nature. Like most believers today, when it came time to give in the church my countenance would fall. If I had been jumping up and down with the excitement of the word that was being preached, this is the one part of the service that would bring me crashing back to 'reality'. I would make sure that I did not give everything that was in my purse even if I could afford to. I would deliberately push away the higher notes in a bid to find coins of lesser value. If none were found, I would give the note but the queen's face on the money would be squeezed so tight that tears would come streaming down her face, as I would be squeezing her so tight instead of dropping the money in the offering basket. I just didn't want to give it. It is no surprise that my relationship with God at that time was nothing to write home about. Its only until I realised my sin that my life as I knew it changed forever. From that time many years ago, I have come a long way. My relationship with God is at a higher level and it keeps growing from strength to strength.

God has told us in His word that if you give you shall receive. This is how Luke puts it,

Luke 6 vs. 38
Give, and it shall be given unto you; good measure, pressed down, and shaken together, and running over, shall men give into your bosom. For with the same measure that ye mete withal it shall be measured to you again.

It is a law that is in motion. If you give you will receive. Just as much as the law of gravity exists so it is with the law of giving. My husband and I have now gotten to a point where we give not because our eyes are solely focused on what God will do for us in return, but because we are lovers by nature that automatically makes us givers by nature. We love what God loves and God loves to give. In fact He gave the most incredible gift that surpasses all others on earth and that is salvation through our Lord Jesus Christ. It was a sacrifice He made for us.

Realise right now that if you ever want to have a relationship with God where He calls you 'friend', you have to be a giver by nature. Be like Abraham who when he realised the favour he had found in the sight of God did not hesitate to give something of his substance. Abraham was also a tither.

Genesis 14 vs. 20
"...And he gave him tithes of all".
Giving is God's way of helping us to love him more. We are the ones who benefit from giving. If we give we receive so that makes us beneficiaries. In the book of Matthew 6:21 Jesus taught that,

"For where your treasure is, there will your heart be also".

If you place the highest value on material things, your heart will automatically follow those material things. If on the other hand, you place the highest value on God's glory and invest in the things of God, then your dearest love will be found in those things as well. I have heard on several occasions' people complain that they feel 'low' spiritually and dry. This happens because of lack of intimacy with God. They may be doing everything right but they do not have a giving nature. My husband often says DEBT stands for "Doing Everything But Tithing". The spiritual passion in you can be revived because you are a giver by nature. You gain intimacy with God because you care for the things he cares for. You pay your tithe and offering because you are a lover and giver by nature, you help the needy around you because it is your nature to give. These are some of the mandates God gave us when it comes to ministering with our substance. You gain intimacy with God if giving is your nature like Abraham.

The Moses kind of bargain

The second patriarch we'll look at who had a tremendously intimate relationship with God is Moses. The book of Exodus says,

Exodus 32 vs. 11-14
"Then Moses pleaded with the Lord and said, `Lord why does your wrath burn hot against your people whom you

have brought out of the land of Egypt with great power and with a mighty hand. Why should the Egyptian speak and say He brought them out to harm them to kill them in the mountains and to consume them from the face of the earth. *Turn from your fierce wrath and relent from the harm to Your people. Remember Abraham, Isaac and Israel, Your servants to whom you swore by Your own self.'* So the Lord relented from the harm which He said He would do to His people."

Wow! Did you see that? This is a remarkable incident. In verse 10 the Lord says,

"Let Me alone that My wrath may burn hot against them that I may consume them."

Here Papa God was angry! When anger burns hot then it's something else! The bible puts it right this way,

Jeremiah 20 vs. 11
"But the LORD [is] with me as a mighty terrible one…"

God was so angry that He wanted to destroy His own people. He actually told Moses, **"Get aside I am coming to destroy them."**

This means the only thing that stood between God and destroying these people instantaneously was Moses. Old Moses was so in touch, so intimate, so attuned to the heartbeat of his God to an extent that he could tell God to 'repent'. He could stand comfortably between millions of people and God.

Moses goes on to say,

"Please don't do it for the sake of our ancestors Abraham, Isaac, Jacob, the covenant that they have made with you. Lord, don't do it. Remember that covenant."

This is remarkable. It shows the degree of intimacy between the Creator and His created. They were intimate. They were best friends; lovers and no one else could ever have done what Moses did. No one else at that time came close to the level of closeness that was between Moses and God. It is in this book that I will show you ways to gain this level of intimacy with God. A level where you know God so well you can 'negotiate' with Him.

Praying your way to intimacy

I remember a time some years ago when my husband and I were called out to pray for someone in a city on the opposite side of England from where we lived. It was going to be a long journey so we decided to retire early in preparation for the trip the following morning. I woke up to find my husband deep in conversation with God and as he concluded, I heard him say, "Lord may you show us a sign of what was to happen".

So we got ready and got into our car and in true Angel tradition we prayed for our awaiting journey. It is then that my husband mentioned to me what God had shown him during the night. He had seen a plot unfold showing what the devil had planned against us. It was a fatal accident that was going to take place at a precise location just a few miles away from our destination. So he had told God to show us a sign of what was to happen.

Now I have to say this is something that should never be attempted if you are not at the right level of intimacy or faith for that matter.

Exactly at the location stated by my husband, one of the tyres on our car burst and was completely shredded potentially causing a serious accident. At that moment, I did not even know something was wrong. I simply thought that my husband was changing lanes yet the tyre had just exploded! It was as if we were carried to the side of the road. As He parked he told me that the Lord had just shown us what was supposed to have happened. By that time two policemen who were passing by pulled over to see what had happened. They were astonished to see the extent of the damage on the tyre. According to them, all accidents they had seen involving tyre bursts of this calibre had been fatal.

So how is it that he could have talked to God and told God that he wanted to see what was to come? How is it that a mere man can speak and God listens and takes action immediately? I want to show you how prayer plays a big role when it comes to growing more intimate with God.

A life of prayer is one of the factors that increase intimacy. There are people who pray and they know without a doubt that their prayers will be answered.

There are three main levels that we are going to look at.

The outer court friend

Like the temple Moses built, prayer has three levels that define the person who is at that particular level. The vast majority of believers reside there. In this level, the believer mostly prays for physical or natural needs. It is hardly ever spiritual. It is always what they don't have and they require God to go and 'fetch' the things they want. This is the believer who goes to church with a specific need and as soon as it is met they leave never to be seen in the house of the Lord again. It is a prayer life that is focused mainly on getting things rather than growing more intimate with God. In the book of Matthew, we are given insight into the time we should spend asking for natural things and the proportion on physical things seems to be quite small.

Matthew 6 vs.33
Seek ye first the kingdom of God and His righteousness and all these things shall be added onto you.

The word of God is placing more emphasis on seeking the Kingdom of God. Spend more time seeking intimacy with Him and loving Him so much that you don't waste your time asking for material things from Him. Even if you look at the Lords prayer, which was an Old Testament prayer there is actually one main verse that covers physical needs. The rest covers other areas. But with the majority of Christians the Outer Court friends' prayer takes most of

Intimacy

their time. This type of friendship does not yield much as it is not based on a real relationship with God. It is mainly born out of need.

I remember a lady who once came to our church. She had a tonne of problems and it seemed to her as if there just was no way out. She told me issues ranging from marriage problems (her husband had just left her) to the few pounds left in her bank account. She had been to different churches for so long seeking help. She had fasted, prayed, praised and even sown seeds to try and alleviate the problems but nothing changed. During this conversation with her, I realised that the main thing that this woman lacked was a love relationship with God. She was not intimate with God. She had gotten so used to the outer court friendship with God that is mainly based on asking for needs to be met rather than getting to know Him better. Her need had completely consumed any desire to become intimate with God. The moment I shared this with her everything about this woman changed. She started coming to the daily prayer meetings held at the church and this time she knew she was seeking a relationship with the real love of her life and best friend. It was not long before one by one everything she had shared with me was completely restored even better than it was before. She had now moved further and accessed what I call the Inner court friendship with God. The first veil had been removed and here she was in the Inner Court friendship with God.

Intimacy

The Inner court friendship

There are those who have managed to go past the first covering and are now praying and seeking God to know the deeper purpose of their lives. They want to know what they were called to do, their personal ministries and how to grow in them. It is more about seeking gifts in this level of friendship. They have developed their prayer life enough to enter into an Inner court friendship with God. This is where the meat of the gospel is desired. It is not the milk level. People who are in the inner court are more concerned about what they can be used of God to do. They just want to be able to impact others lives.

The danger is we also find a lot of 'religious' folk here too. They seek gifts for the wrong reasons; they like to prove they are no longer in the outer court all for the wrong reasons. They are like the seniors in school who liked to show that they were way ahead of you if you were just starting out. If only they could let go of self-importance their friendship with God has so much potential to grow into something deeper.

There is a young man my husband and I met not too long ago who is a classic example of someone who is in the inner court. We could see that he was someone who had zeal for the things of God especially ministry gifts and gifts of the Spirit. He really wanted to be used by God but the only problem was it was all for the wrong reasons. He had this air of 'knowing it all'. He would come to us with various questions and the moment we tried to answer, he would start preaching to us! The man also had a host of problems but he just could not stop to listen. We never could say anything to him. If we tried to give him scriptures to meditate on, he would start shouting back the references before we got the chance to say them and even quote more on top of ours!

He was positioned well in the inner court and had a bigger opportunity to become a good friend of God as he advanced in an intimate relationship with God. He could have let go of pride and taken advantage of the fact that he was already in the inner court and start romancing the heart of God.

This book is meant to create in you a deeper walk with the Lord. Intimacy that produces a kind of buzzing excited love that makes you nervous in the right sense. Intimacy that creates in you a desire to not just be an inner court friend of God but to go further into the Most Holy place (holy of holies) kind of friendship.

Most Holy Place (Holy of holies) friendship

This level of intimacy built through prayer is the highest level possible. It is a level of prayer that is not seeking anything. Its not about material things, it's not about acquiring any spiritual gifts but it's all about intimate time spent with God. The truly intimate friends of God reside in this level of prayer.

If you look at Abraham and Moses, you will begin to see a similarity in their walk with God and I will be showing you through the pages of this book the qualities they exuded that will help you to gain an intimate relationship with God. This is tried and tested. My husband and I have experienced the word of God. The words have jumped out of the bible and straight into our day-to-day lives. We have handled this word of truth and gained intimacy with our Lord praise God!

These two men gave up everything so that God could be their only source. By so doing you can already see that they had since moved from the outer court type of friendship with God that always seeks material things.

Genesis 12.Vs 1
Get thee out of the land, get out of your kinsfolk and go to the land, which I call you to.

Abraham left everything. On your journey to intimacy with God, you need to let go of self. Get to a position where you can tell God that even if I lose everything, I will still love you the same. Material things do not compare to your relationship with God. Job never let go of his love for God. Even though he was left in the gutters after having lived a lavish lifestyle, he never wavered in his love of God. We all know how Job's story ends- acquiring wealth and blessings that far surpassed what he had initially. See that? Are you able to come to a position where you just love God even if your bank account has accumulated cobwebs? To love Him even if you are single yet age forty is fast approaching? To love God even when your husband is messing with Chequita and Channeyney? To love Him even if the child you have always wanted has no yet manifested and the in-laws are wagging their tongues? Will you still stand and give a shout out to your lover and friend the Most High God?

Intimacy is all about sacrifice. It's about leaving everything and going in hot pursuit of the one and only love of your life. It's about blind faith that tells you He has your back even if you don't 'feel' Him close to you all the time. To be so in love with God that you don't care about much except your love life with Him. We read shortly afterwards in genesis 14 how God blessed Abraham.

Genesis 14. Vs 19
"…Melchizedek came and blessed him…"

Abraham was now at a level of romancing the heart of God that he had no business asking God for anything. He already knew that God was his source. He saw no need to spend hours as an outer court friend asking for material things, his intimacy with the Lord was on a most holy place level. It is an intimacy level where you become one of God's closest friends. He didn't ask God to provide the car he was going to use to go out and preach the gospel or the suits he was to wear as he led the people of God. He just blindly stepped out of his house by faith and started moving knowing that God had already provided.

Abraham depended solely on God. He had no plan 'B' like most Christians in church now. They always figure that if they go on a hundred day fast, forty more days than last year, their miracle should be able to show up. If it doesn't this time, they know they can always move on to a plan 'B' which they will have formulated in their minds.

I once overheard a conversation in a certain church some years ago where I had been invited to a conference. The speaker had just completed the service and the people gathered around tables for refreshments. It is at this point that I overheard a group of women on the opposite table discussing about marriage. The older women were advising a younger woman on how she should go about it if her boyfriend did not propose. They came up will all sorts of suggestions on how to corner the guy but finally the younger lady spoke up and said,

" I don't care what happens now. By October if I am not married then I will make sure that I am pregnant if not by him then by someone else".

To my utter amazement, the older women were in favour of this plan B! What a mess!

This is what we have in churches. This lady had convinced herself that if the right channels do not work, then she would go for the back up plan. Back-up plans do not work with God. You either believe He has done it for you or you don't.

Intimacy

Abraham had no plan 'B'. He looked to God as his best friend and no one else. He even said in the book of Genesis 14 vs. 22-23,

"And Abram said to the King of Sodom, I have lift up mine hand unto the LORD, the most high God, the possessor of heaven and earth, that I will not take from a thread even to a shoe latchet, and that I will not take any thing is thine, lest thou shouldest say, I have made Abram rich."

Abraham was so intimate with God he couldn't bear the fact that anyone else besides God would take the credit that they had made him rich. With the "possessor of heaven and earth" as his best friend, surely he had nothing to worry about. He also made a decision not to have anything but what God gives. He had managed to feel the 'heartbeat' of God and move according to God's rhythm. He is an Old Testament man who managed to go out of the outer court into a deeper new covenant type of relationship with God. We are in the new covenant. Christ has taken up residence in us. Your friendship with God should be greater than the Old Testament folk because Christ lives in us.

Your best friend as your defence

Moses was such a humble man before God and this was one of his most striking characteristics. Nowadays we have people who go around telling people "I am a humble man or woman of God". A truly humble person does not really know they are. Even when they are told they are humble it almost shocks them or almost embarrasses them. It comes as news to them. When you are humble you have a heart for the things of God. You are determined to learn more about this God we serve. You have a desire to draw closer and closer to Him. You desire to know Him intimately by having full access to His secrets. Look at what God did in defence of His friend Moses. In verse 6, God told Aaron,

"Hear now my words if there is a prophet in your nation, I make myself Known to him in a vision and I speak to him in a dream. Not so with My servant Moses. He is faithful in all my house. I speak with him face to face even plainly and not in dark saying and he sees the form of the Lord. Why then were you not afraid to speak against my servant Moses?"

Moses was standing in the office of a Prophet at that time. God then comes and interjects defending His own best friend praise God!

God even went further to say Moses was not only a prophet but also a good friend of His. Wouldn't you want to have such an intimate relationship with God that you have Him on your corner always? He is your defence when all else seems to have failed you.

Prophet Victor Boateng is my husbands' father and mentor. He tells of an incident where at one time he was one of the most persecuted Prophets in Ghana on a popular radio station. A certain DJ just hated the way God was using him.

Intimacy

So he would slander the prophet on the air any time he got a free moment to do so.

A day came when one day the prophet was driving home and a terrible storm suddenly broke out. As he was driving he noticed someone who was stranded by the roadside and as he usually does he pulled over to help. Little did he know that the person he was helping was the DJ who had been slandering him on live radio. The DJ himself did not realise that this was the prophet he always spoke bad of on radio. Prophet Victor then made a few calls to the relevant people who came to the roadside immediately to assist the man. After some time the DJ found out that the person who had helped him when he needed help the most was the same person he had hated for no reason. He headed straight for the church where the prophet was ministering and knelt down crying and asking for forgiveness.

God had come to the defence of his friend. Prophet Victor didn't have to say anything in retaliation; God fought the war for him. This is what happens when your relationship with God becomes intimate. He becomes your defence no matter what happens. People will speak against you, persecute you just always remember that He is your defence. As you ignore persecution you gain intimacy with God because you allow Him to be your defence and good friends defend each other. You will face financial persecution in your household or in your business but again, God is your defence.

Intimacy

II Chronicles 20:15
"...for the battle is not yours, but God's..."

Notice that Moses had gone against what God had said. If you read the story in its entirety, you will see that his sister Mirriam was right in a way to try and correct her brother. The irony however of the whole matter is that God came to the defence of His servant. Despite the fact that his siblings might have been right in their judgement, in the sight of God it was unheard of to speak against His best friend. It was just not acceptable to speak against His prophet.

See, God becomes your defence. He says it in His word that he will fight our battles for us.

Desire to love and be a lover of God. To be so intimate with Him that you get to a level where you see Him face to face and have meetings with him.

My husband has seen the lord Jesus Christ seven times to date as the Lord came into his room and sat down to discuss things. This is the holy of holies type of relationship with God. When you become intimate with Him, there is a strong spiritual magnetic force that causes God to turn His face in favour upon you. Some have asked my husband why God chose him to do the things he does and he always replies "Why not me?" Your character draws God to you. You find favour in His sight.

God desires that we get to know Him better. To get to a level where we know how to romance his heart and become best friends with Him.

Intimacy

James 4 vs. 8
Draw nigh to God and He will draw nigh unto you.

God caused Moses to have a good rapport. I am giving you secrets that will bring God's attention to you and gain a friendship unlike any other. We have handled this word of truth my husband and I and we now know that His word is real. Learn from the principles quantified in this book, start romancing the heart of God and become his best friend.

Take a look at Apostle Paul. Because of intimacy obtained through romancing the heart of God, he could get a lot of revelations and miracles, signs and wonders to happen. Signs, miracles and wonders became an everyday reality because there was oneness between Apostle Paul and the Lord that went beyond other normal relationships. Apostle Paul had touched the pulse of God through time spent building a strong intimate relationship.

Notice the time when the Macedonian, call took place. Apostle Paul was headed for Asia but because of intimacy he had the ability to know when God had changed the route to Macedonia.

Acts 16 vs. 9
And a vision appeared to Paul in the night; there stood a man of Macedonia, and prayed him, saying, come over into Macedonia, and help us.

It might have been in a dream but somehow he was convinced God had already spoken. A lot of people take dreams lightly and if the Apostle was not intimate with God he would most probably have brushed it off like most people do their dreams. The urgency by which he responded proves that 'romancing' the heart of his God pushed him into realising the urgency in the dream. Upon realising this, he turned the ship around and also his crew around to go to Macedonia. See, he did not care what the Macedonians were going to say or whether they were going to receive him or not. All he knew was the pulse of God indicated that Macedonia needed a word and he took the opportunity and ran with it. That only happens when a man is holding the pulse of God. It can only takes place when a man is in touch with what God wants at a particular moment, time and place.

Romancing the heart of God carries principles that will turn the average Christian into a hot believer who burns for the Lord. Loving and befriending God is easy, it only requires one to learn principles that people who were friends of God used.

Notice Moses telling God to 'repent' from His anger. He actually said,

Exodus 32 vs. 12
"...repent from your anger..."

How can Moses tell God to repent? How? It's because lovers and friends can gain access that allows them to say some things the average Christian cannot say.

Intimacy

What about Abraham who could stand before God and negotiate? What gave him the right to negotiate with the living God? Was he not afraid? Did he not understand who the Lord was? How can he negotiate with a God, who says,

Malachi 3 vs. 6
"For I am the LORD, I change not..."

What entered into Moses and Abraham that they could negotiate with God as a man negotiates with business partners? Had they lost their minds? Was something wrong in their brains or their lives? How can a mortal stand to negotiate with God? One thing is for sure. It was because they had a relationship that went past being believers and yes, they had touched the pulse of God. They had 'romanced' His heart through their lives. They had embraced the heart of the creator.

See what God did when Moses said,

Exodus 32 vs. 12
"...repent from your anger..."

The bible has the audacity to tell us a couple of verses later:

Exodus 32 vs. 14
"...AND God repented from His anger"

What? God listened to Moses and repented! Did we read that right? Yes we did!

Intimacy

There was something greater here than what meets the eye. These men had a tangible history with God even there in the Old Testament to such an extent that Abraham was called a friend of God. Even now Heaven itself is still called 'Abrahams bosom'. It is called the belly of Abraham because the man knew how to genuinely 'romance' the heart of his God Jehovah. He knew how to get God to be a lover and a dear friend. That is what many Christians today are failing to do and when they see those whom God has chosen to use as His lovers and best friend they start persecuting.

Many who are persecuted are opposed because they have a deeper walk with God that guarantees them a lot of things that are extraordinary to the human eye. So people noticing the extraordinary power in them think the devil is at work. Why? They have spent years praying for God to use them but there seems to be no answer to their prayers. They are as weak as when they started fasting and praying because in all their toil to get power or a miracle no one taught them the power behind intimacy, romancing the heart of God.

That is the purpose of this book, to outline the many principles that get the Christian or the believer into a lover and a best friend of God!

To be in love and to love

There is a big difference between being in love and loving. That is part of the difficult parts of understanding what this book is about. This message is not meant to show you just how to love but how to be in love. See, these are those that love God and there are those who are IN LOVE WITH GOD. The only problem we see today and why believers are no longer carriers of signs, miracles and wonders is simply because some are just Christians, some are lovers but few are IN LOVE WITH GOD. In other words there is no 'romance' left in their walk with God.

To love is to cherish, respect, to want to know better and also other things BUT to be IN LOVE is to never want to let go for whatever the reason. It is to share intimate feelings, hopes and dreams. It is to feel so passionate and excited that you won't take your eyes off your lover. It is to seek to understand your lover rather than want to be understood. To be IN LOVE is deeper than just to love. Loving also is deeper than just being a believer as many are today.

To love and to be in love with God are both important but not the same. They share some characteristics but are not the same. To be in love is way deeper than just simply loving someone. God wants us to really be in love with Him. He yearns for intimacy. He wants His creation to break through the veil and cuddle Him in glory. This is hard for the religious minds but God wants His creation to get deeper with Him, to get into real deep love. God wants us to 'romance' His heart. God wants us to love what he loves, hate what He hates not because it's written but because we are in love with Him, our will changes to His will. He wants it to be so, so that our will changes not because He wants us to change them only but because there is something in Him and in us that is now knit together because of intimacy that calls for it. Being in love should be the reason why my will changes.

Now, when you are in love with God you do not change your ways just because you know God hates your bad ways. No, not one bit. You change because that's the way you just find yourself thinking as you melt into His arms with love. When deep love gotten through 'romancing' His heart comes, you will find yourself struggling for words because of love. You will find yourself finishing each other's sentences with God. You will find yourself with a new song in your spirit everyday because you are now knit together for you are IN LOVE. Romancing God's heart makes it easy to follow God's commandments. No wonder the Lord Jesus Christ used to be moved by love (compassion).

Matthew 9 vs. 36
But when He saw the multitudes, He was *moved with Compassion on them*, because they fainted, and were Scattered abroad, as sheep having no shepherd.

Notice the word compassion and notice that it is love that pushed Him. He would heal because love pushed Him to. The word compassion itself goes miles deeper than what I am outlining here. My husband has a book called,"The Hidden Secret to Releasing the Power of God". In this book he reveals revelation knowledge that has a lot to do with compassion.

So going back to The Lord Jesus, He would do good deeds because love compelled Him. See, when you are in love,

love pushes you into miracles, signs and wonders. You no longer do good because you ought to but because you love to. You don't think like the old you but you just find yourself thinking the right way because you have 'romanced' God's heart! It's crucial to have this intimacy with God and know exactly how to be a friend of God. He should be our best friend who is closer to us than we are to ourselves. He is a friend who only is interested in my development as a believer. One who wants me to prosper and inspires, motivates me to have the best future. He says so plainly in His word,

Jeremiah 29:11
I know the plans I have for you,' declares the Lord, 'plans to prosper you and not to harm you, plans to give you hope and a future.

I want us now to look at one of my favorite principles that lead to romancing the heart of God and that is worship. I will show you how deep dimensions of worship can get you straight into the throne room of God and a whole you new facet of intimacy.

The Levels of Worship

Worship is the bedrock of romancing the heart of God. It is the essence of a romantic relationship with Him. It is the adoration part where we cannot take our eyes off the love of our life. It is the fragrance that makes up our relationship with Him. The tender moments spent in complete and utter awe of Him. It is that hard to explain feeling that you get when you are so deep in love that no one else can understand even if you try to explain.

I want you to take a look at what the bible says about worship so that you can get the essence of what worship fully involves. If you already had information on what you think worship is the best thing is to empty your cup so that you can receive. It is impossible to fill up a cup that is already full.

Among the many words that define what worship truly is, I am going to highlight only a few from the bible that I know will elevate your understanding to another level in your intimate walk with God. These are a combination of Hebrew and Greek words that define worship. Some of the words are things we do and some things God expects from us. I have outlined these starting with proskuneo.

Proskuneo

The Lord Jesus Christ says this to the woman at the well,

John 4 vs. 21-23
Jesus said to her,"Woman believe Me the hour is coming when you will neither on this mountain nor in Jerusalem worship the Father. You worship what you do not know; we know what we worship, for salvation is of the Jews. But the hour is coming, and now is, when the *true worshippers will worship the Father in spirit and truth for the Father is seeking such to worship Him.*

The word worship is repeated a total of six times in the passages above and all have the same meaning in the Greek, which is Proskuneo, **to kiss toward or to lean forward so as to kiss and then ends with kissing.**

The book of Matthew 2 vs. 9 speaks of the wise men,

"...**When they saw the star, they rejoiced with exceeding great joy. And when they had come into the house, they saw the young Child with Mary His mother, and** *fell down and worshiped Him.* **And when they had opened their treasures, they presented gifts to Him gold, frankincense and myrrh."**

When the wise men saw their new King and savior, they worshipped Him. The gifts they gave to Him were the *result* of worship. We confuse between the result of worship and the spirit of worship. Some people when they come to church, they experience the power of God and His glory so much that they fall down and worship Him. As a result they are pushed to give God something. You can give those gifts in the house of God but if those gifts come from pride, worship is automatically gone out the window.

Note that the Hebrew word for worship *shachah* is similar to the Greek word for worship, which we are looking at now - *proskuneo*. Both of them include the act of bowing down. This however is a brief outline of some of the levels of worship. Otherwise it takes an entire book to cover everything comprehensively!

Worshiping includes singing unto The Lord but when it is not from a humble heart, worship in its essence disappears completely. There is a couple Papa Kenneth Hagin, our spiritual father, spoke of who were leading a worship session one time in a certain church. They had wonderful voices that could hit all the difficult notes with such ease. Everyone in the room was excited and they ululated and clapped as the couple demonstrated perfected voices in worship. After they were done singing their worship item, an old couple came up to the stage with only a guitar and they begin to sing unto the Lord. Their voices were very shaky and they certainly could not hit any high note. Some notes were out of tune but a phenomenal thing happened shortly after they started. Every single person in the room was knocked out completely under the glory of God as some wept and others knelt at the alter repenting of their wrongdoings.

See that? If worship is done in truth and in spirit – it is vindicated. If pride sets in and all we care about is hitting the right notes and sounding good to the people, the spirit of worship lifts.

The whole idea is to be humble in the presence of God. You can sing, dance and shout all you like but if your motive is not right then its wrong.

There is a man I saw once dancing as if mad in the house of the Lord. The man brought out of the bag every style of dance as he danced and danced in worship. It seemed he didn't care who was watching all he cared to do was dance for his God.

Afterwards I had people approaching me to report that they found his style of dancing 'offensive'. They wanted him to be reproached for dancing in such an offensive way! Listen, however you worship God if it is in spirit and in truth then its correct. David danced until he became naked!

2 Samuel 6 vs. 14
"And David danced before the LORD with all his might; and David was girded with a linen ephod."

Vs. 16 goes on to say,
"...Michal Saul's daughter looked through a window, and

saw king David leaping and dancing before the LORD; and she despised him in her heart."

You see David was in a deep level of worship that he didn't care about whether the handmaidens were looking or not. His wife Michal is the one who decided to be the voice of reason and advise him that what he had done was wrong. And David rightfully answered,

2 Samuel 6 vs. 21
"...It was before the LORD, which chose me before thy father... therefore will I play before the LORD.
Worshiping God is showing Him humility. The wise men showed humility as they bowed down before Him and worshipped Him.

Proskuneo is leaning forward and kissing the master's feet. It is humiliating to kiss someone's feet. You feel so small and powerless yet that's proskuneo. You are bowing down unashamedly and kissing Jesus feet.

We sometimes have some seriously powerful worship sessions in our church and demons can't help themselves but check out in such an atmosphere. We have people lying prostate on the ground, some laughing, some crying out to God and some lying motionless for hours. It's a tangible atmosphere where some have seen open visions while in this state. It's a deeper worship that allows you to romance the heart of God and gain access into His secrets. But you see in all this glory, there are some proud people that I have seen standing and biting their nails! They cannot bear to be

Intimacy

seen looking vulnerable. Talk about insensitivity to the Spirit of God!

We are talking about how to humble ourselves before God and thus experience a close friendship with God. *Proskuneo* speaks about humbling of our heart, our mind, of changing our mindset before God and allowing Him to do whatever He sees fit in us. It is allowing Him access into out hearts and going deeper into an intimate relationship with Him. That is the meaning and definition of worship.

Segad

The first word in the Hebrew describing worship is ***segad**- to bow before Him.*

Dan. 3 vs.4
"… O peoples, nations and languages that at the time you hear the sound of the horn, flute, harp, lyre and psaltery, in symphony with all kinds of music, you shall fall down and *worship* the gold image that King Nebuchadnezzar has set up…"

You see the words that describe worship are different depending on the context. Shachah and proskuneo also include among other things bowing down just like segad. The difference is *segad* means to bow down and pay respect to a notable person or somebody higher than yourself and ***it may not include your heart***. It only physically refers to your body posture. I am sure at the time of Daniel a lot of

Intimacy

people in Nebuchadnezzar's kingdom didn't really want to bow before those idols. They did it unwillingly out of fear. There were serious repercussions if anyone didn't bow down.

The word s*egad* is never used in a true sense of worship to our God. This tells us that God doesn't just want our outward form, our outward worship, our physical worship or posture alone although the words *shachah* and *proskuneo* include that but they go beyond just bowing before God. With these two, it's all about romancing the heart of God. It's all about intimacy.

A lot of people in church today 'segad'. They like to show that they are close to God by their body postures. They will 'act out' true worship. God is not looking for just actions; He wants us to have a relationship with Him that allows us to gain access into His secrets. You see, God is a gentleman; He wants us to bow down to Him willingly because we love Him. It is not His intention to force anyone to love Him. We bow because we are intimate. The purpose for knowing segad is for you to be aware that as you seek a deeper relationship with God through worship, you cease to act out things and worship Him in truth and in Spirit.

Atsab

Atsab is a worldly form of worship. If we take a look at the book of Jeremiah it becomes clearer.

Jeremiah 44:19
"...And when we burned incense to the queen of heaven and poured out drink offerings to her, did we make cakes for her, to *worship (atsab)* her, and pour out drink offerings to her without our husbands' permission?"

Here is a worldly form of worship. Atsab involves worshipping of things like the sun, moon and trees.

The women mentioned in the above scripture were in atsab. In *atsab* worship you worship with things. It can be an incense offering.

Notice that tithes and offerings are part of our worship. As I explained the wise men gave Jesus gifts after they had worshipped Him in truth and in spirit.

Some people think that worshipping God means to give Him something. If that's our thinking, we only understand *atsab* worship and not *shachah or proskuneo* worship. Some may say that they don't burn incense or include objects when they worship God in church but the fact of the matter is if we think in our heart that doing something for God or giving God something is the essence of worship, then we are reducing worship to atsab worship – worldly worship. God is not after your money. He wants your life; He wants to have an intimate relationship with you. The essence of worship is love. It's not in acting like we love Him or in giving all sorts of gifts without love. When He has your life and He becomes your Lord, you automatically surrender your tithes and offerings to Him. This is the result of your relationship with God. You become a giver because you love God not as an act of worship that stands alone.

Shachah

As we have seen, shachah and proskuneo are similar. Now lets look at the word *shachah* in detail.

Genesis 22 vs.5
"And Abraham said to his young men. "Stay here with the donkey, the lad and I will go yonder and *worship*, and we will come back to you."

The word here used is the Hebrew word *shachah*, which means to bow down **yourself**. Notice that it is entirely different from *segad*. *Segad* means to bow down only, whereas *shachah* means to *bow down **yourself***. Remember we looked at Daniel chapter 3 and everyone was bowing down but it was not out of reverence but fear. They knew that if they didn't bow they would be thrown into the fiery furnace. In Genesis 22, Abraham took the son himself; Abraham bound the son himself; Abraham sought to sacrifice the son himself. God never did it for him. God simply gave the instruction and Abraham did the rest *by himself*. He worshipped God willingly. It was not a forcing matter. He had gotten to a level where he trusted God enough to simply follow what he had been told willingly.

Shachah speaks of something deeper. Worship in its essence means to humble ourselves before God. If we acknowledge

Intimacy

that we need Him and useless without Him we open doors to enter into a deeper level.

I want to share with you an incident that took place as I was in the middle of writing this book. On this day, I had spent all day focusing on the content of 'Intimacy' when I asked the Lord if I could have an 'intimate experience' based on the principles outlined in the book. Now again, asking such things depends on how close you are to God. You should not be in the habit of asking God to show you things to prove Himself. The bible says that you are blessed if you believe without seeing. And there is also a danger of the devil giving you 'an experience' and you start thinking it was God.

As night fell, I went up to my room not expecting anything to happen. I knelt down to pray as usual and as I was praying, I suddenly felt myself moving and when I opened my eyes I noticed that I was floating centimeters in the air. I tried to stand up but it seemed as if something extremely powerful was keeping me in that stance. Before I could do anything it seemed as if I slipped into another dimension and I couldn't keep my eyes open. The moment I did seconds later, I found myself in a beautiful, captivating, enchanting forest and an angel of the Lord was standing there with my husband as if they were expecting me.

The angel of the Lord then spoke and said 'welcome to Heaven'. I almost jumped out of my skin, as I knew I was conscious and this was really happening. My husband took my hand and we started walking with this majestic angel and they began to show me an amazing 'project' that was taking place in Heaven. It was like a construction site with no machinery. Only invisible hands gently moving things around ever so gently and leisurely. The angel of the Lord then spoke and said this was a site that was being prepared to build more mansions for those who love God! Praise the Lord for His mercy endures forever!

Intimacy is real. God is as real as you are to yourself. You need to access another dimension of intimacy with Him – He has always been ready and willing.

Start today. Worship is in your heart. You could do *segad*, you could bow down and your heart could still have pride. You could *atsab* or give something like the Pharisees and the Sadducees who gave things to the temple but they had pride in their hearts.

You can give God your tithes of thousands of dollars and it means nothing if your heart is proud - there is no worship. You can sing the loudest, play music instruments the most skillfully but if you are not humble, there is no worship. Pride is the very opposite of the essence of worship. And God will not have any other gods before Him.

Papa Victor K. Boateng, the man God gave us in a vision as a mentor and a father, after the going to glory of Papa Kenneth Hagin, is a deep worshipper bar none. When he worships he quickly loses track of time. Its like he will be consumed by the love that he sees before the Lord. At one time he worshipped and fasted for a whole year. Here I am talking of dry fast, all because real worship hides your pain and your hunger. In fact it fills your belly.

Papa Victor K. Boateng could not speak English, did not go to school like many people do, but after the full year of fasting, he just realized that God had touched his tongue when he found himself speaking fluent English. It's like he worshipped himself into understanding the English language. One minute you cant speak English and the next you are an expert in a language you did not even learn. That's what shacha can do.

In a nutshell, the essence of worship is a humble heart. A heart that is willing to get to know God more.

Chapter Three

The Art of Surrendering

Galatians 2 vs. 20
"I am crucified with Christ, nevertheless I live, yet Not I but Christ Lives in me…"

When we started our ministry we received a lot of persecution that it was simply hard to understand why. Until the Lord told us that we needed to surrender all including our pride so as to be with Him. We did and God's love replaced our dignity and integrity that we didn't care what people said or did. We still don't.

Now, what is this issue of surrendering all anyway? Apostle Paul seemed to have gotten a grasp of it and yet it is part of the things one does to be sure intimacy with God works. Apostle Paul says he lost all things in order to gain intimacy with the Lord. Notice here,

Philippians 3 vs. 8
"…I consider everything a loss compared to the surpassing Greatness of knowing Christ Jesus my Lord, for whose sake I have lost all things…"

You see that if you are joined to Christ the owner of everything it means it does not hurt to lose everything because losing everything means gaining everything. How? Because when I lose what I own and join myself to the one I love who has everything, that means I have just exchanged what I lost for what He has and that instantly makes me a rich person.

Intimacy requires casting all your burdens on Christ and never to deal with them yourself.

Your heart should embrace freedom

Your heart should embrace freedom by adopting an "I don't care" attitude. Your heart should realize what you can't change and what only God can change. Notice the scripture,

Philippians 4 vs. 6
"Be careful for nothing…"

The word says, "Be careful for nothing" meaning to say we should never be found anxious. I remember days when I had not known intimacy, how I used to be troubled by small issues and problems. I remember many sleepless nights. Nights spent wondering what tomorrow was to bring. I could not wait for tomorrow. I worried and worried but God spoke and said, "Cast your cares upon me" just as it is stated in the word in the book of psalm,

Psalm 55 vs. 22
Cast your cares on the LORD and he will sustain you, he will never let the righteous be shaken".

You see worry gets people depressed. Worry kills the ability of a believer to be intimate because intimacy involves trust. If one trusts the one they love then if the one they love is God and they are intimate with Him, He will provide before they even ask. He would provide before they even know He has done it. Where there is intimacy there is an ability to trust and when trust is there, there is no sleepless night or anxiousness.

To surrender means to yield ownership, to relinquish control over what we consider ours. When people hear the word surrender they never associate it with positive actions. They always link it to the negative action as in when an enemy surrenders everything after being defeated in battle. This definition and understanding is in the mind of a believer who has not known intimacy. It is a believer who is still immature who considers surrender to mean just giving up control.

When we surrender to God we are simply acknowledging that we are not our own. We belong to Him and without Him we are nothing.

1 Corinthians 6 vs. 19
"...and ye are not your own..."

We acknowledge that what we own belongs to Him and the bad that we do should be thrown out of the window as we take the good that He is. God is the giver of all things.

Surrender is a choice

Adam and Eve were never told "You CANNOT" they were told you **shall not,** which means they had a choice either to take the fruit or not. They had a choice to eat or not to eat and ultimately they had a greater choice to surrender the lusts of their hearts to God even way before the devil 'beguiled' Eve as she put it. They did not. They failed to surrender their lusts to the God who created them therefore removing their intimacy. They ignored intimacy by failing to make their desires God's desires. They failed to understand that there was no difference between what was theirs and what belonged to God. All things belonged to God including Adam and Eve but Adam and Eve did not know it. They acted like they belonged to themselves.

Had Adam and Eve chosen to follow God by totally surrendering and trusting Him we would have had an easier way of hearing God's voice. However one man and one woman's failure to be intimate caused the rest of humanity to be chased out of the garden where they could have found perfect eternal intimacy. Notice what the Bible says,

Romans 5 vs. 15
"For if through the sin of one many be dead, much more The grace of God, and the gift by grace, which is by one man, Jesus Christ, abounded unto many (by one man salvation came)"

You see, in the Old Testament we see Adam and Eve in the garden and failing to be intimate with God. Then we get

Intimacy

to the New Testament we see the Lord in the garden preparing to die so we can regain access in the garden of intimacy. One man's failure was being cancelled and has been cancelled by one man's success in the garden. God now opened a door for us to be intimate. He opened a huge gate for us to practice intimacy for the practice of intimacy is the practice of heaven and eternity.

Notice it is a choice so never get hung up on opposing Adam and Eve. This is a choice you can make today. You can tell yourself that you are ready to be a deeper lover of God and a best friend of God. You can choose to be captivated by His love. You can choose to reach a level in and with God where as we say – you finish each other's sentences. This is possible today. Nothing can stop you if you get to practice the art of surrendering.

Do Not Worry

Learn not to worry. The Bible says,

Matthew 6 vs. 34
"...tomorrow will worry for itself..."

It is a person who is fully surrendered to God through intimacy that can speak like this. I have met too many people who worry constantly. Worry is simply not trusting God and that is a sin. Other people cannot utter the words "tomorrow will worry about itself". In fact the Bible goes further. It says,

Matthew 6 vs. 27
"shall you add one cubit to your stature by worrying...?"

The Bible tells you that it is difficult and utterly impossible to get anything through worrying. The Bible makes it clear that worrying is not permitted in the intimate zone. A life that has been spent on romancing the heart of God to create intimacy is never perturbed or surprised. It is very still because it knows the words of its lover that say;

Hebrews 13 vs. 5
"...I will never leave you nor forsake you..."

Surrendering will become easier because of this promise.

I remember way back when I was still maturing in intimacy with God, a man approached my husband, Prophet Uebert Angel (you see I have to specify who my husband is so you know he's so taken and so am I). Anyway the man came and said,

"Man of God, I know you're always with your wife but today for the first time I've seen you alone with absolutely no one!"

At this, my husband was genuinely surprised at the statement and I know among the many times that we move around together, that afternoon we were indeed not together. At first as my husband was telling me this, I couldn't understand why he had been seriously and genuinely surprised at the gentleman's statement until I

Intimacy

heard the answer. He said, "Sir you are shortsighted, I am never alone". My husband answered him. "The Lord said He will never leave me nor forsake me. I was with the Lord in the car though you saw me only. You are shortsighted spiritually," my husband continued!

I realized that his life was full of intimacy with His creator and that was why God would speak to Him about events about to unfold in the world with great accuracy. It was all because real lovers and real friends share secrets. God shares His secrets with my husband not only because he is in a prophetic office by calling but it's also because he has learnt the art of intimacy. Prophet Uebert is constantly speaking to God and surrendering his will to God. I am privileged to have seen the spiritual as this man prays. I have seen angels and I have seen the glory cloud on several occasions because of the intimacy that he has learnt to flow in. Some lines from a couple of his favorite worship songs go something like this,

"All that thrills my soul is Jesus; He is more than life to me. And the fairest of ten thousand, in my blessed Lord I see. AND

Forever you will be the lamb upon the throne. I gladly bow my knees, to worship you my Lord!

He sees God as his best friend and also as his father, master and also lover. That is intimacy.

In Africa the glory cloud

In one of our visits to Africa, Zimbabwe, the Lord came early in the morning as we 'romanced' the heart of God through prayer and worship and told us that we were going to be enveloped in the glory cloud. We did not expect anything to happen than we expected to be the first people to land on the moon. That afternoon we held a new members service and right there in front of the 120 new members to the church a thick smoke rose in the room that even the fire authority and the security were called. They searched for the fire but found nothing.

The fire was coming from the room we were having our service in and everyone was panicking yet prophet Uebert kept on smiling and teaching the people. He even told them not to worry about the fire.

When the authorities failed to find the fire, they were surprised because the smoke kept growing in intensity but there was no fire anywhere. It was then that prophet said "This is why I was saying when we first noticed the smoke that it's not what you think it is, but people kept on looking for a fire that only God gives to those who don't just love Him but are in love with Him".

As you surrender to God completely and acknowledge that you are His through and through, you need to embark on an expedition of purity. You cannot be close to God and hold fast to sin. There are three kinds of purity that I would like to share with you that if you just apply these, you will be well on your way as a friend of God. Remember that everything in this book has been tried and tested. Its not just theory that I woke up and thought would play well with the rest of the book. We have done it and it works.

Three kinds of purity that draw you closer to God

For one to be able to feel what God feels. See what God sees, love what God loves and hate what He hates there is a degree of purity that you have to live up to. It is life that is spent in tender intimate moments with God. The word of God speaks of goodness which is also much related to purity in the person. Purity and goodness have a close link that one cannot be good unless they are pure. There is no way one can say that they are good unless they are pure. Now a lot of people tend to think that purity is unachievable. I have often heard some people say that it is actually impossible. Some even go as far as quoting the scripture that says;

Romans 3 vs. 23
We all fall short of the glory of God
What they forget is that the same Bible also says Christ is only coming back for a bride that is pure and holy.

"…to present her to himself as a radiant church,
 without stain or wrinkle or any other blemish,
 but holy and blameless." Eph. 5 vs. 25-27

We may fall short but in Christ we are perfected. He already has a solution for our falling short. The Bible says we are gently bathed in the sweet scented water of the word. In the same book of Ephesians, same chapter 5 vs. 26 says

Intimacy

"...cleansing her by the washing with water through the word"

Purity is achievable because God makes us able. He is the one who cleanses us through the word. He is willing to have an intimate relationship with us. The book of James chapter 4 vs. 8a says;

"Draw nigh to God, and He will draw nigh to you"

Notice that the scripture says we should draw nigh to God first **then** God will draw nigh to us. We initiate the closeness. We get the romance going. We are the ones who determine whether He draws nigh to us.

There are three levels/kinds of goodness/purity that I would like to share with you so you need to stay with this thought.

The first kind of purity

There are three Greek words for purity. Now don't get too caught up with the Greek I just need to go back to the original sense of the word, as this is where the revelation lies. The first one here I want to deal with is '**Katharos'**, which means to be cleansed or washed. It carries the same meaning like our English word *pure*. It's an undefiled purity with no speck of impurity whatsoever. It is used as in a *pure* heart or a *clean* heart. This is the beginning of purity, the purity of the heart. You see there is also the purity of the soul

Intimacy

and that of the body, believe it or not. Katharos talks of the purity of the heart. **It is the same Greek word that Jesus used in John 15: 3**

"You are already katharos (cleansed or washed) because of the Word which I have spoken to you."

See that? You are already clean. The Lord Jesus here knows that He is talking about believers so he uses the word katharos and says you are already katharos meaning to say there is nothing here you can do to be katharos (cleansed) unless he katharoses you himself! Do you get it? As a Christian He has already katharosed (cleansed/washed) you through his word when He saved you. Jesus spent three years cleaning them up by teaching them. They became intimate. They were friends with the Lord. So the only thing we need to do is learn from His word because it is katharosing us every time we read it. We become good. We become pure. We become intimate with God because we are now getting more acquainted with the word of God.

The teaching of the Lord makes us good by making us pure in our hearts. It removes us from adhering to the wrong things. If then we want to be good, we would need purity of the heart. Christ is the word and The Word teaching us will katharos us so we can be good!

The second kind of purity

The other word here for purity is *'eilikrines'*. It also means transparency. This word is a combination of two words, which are 'eili' and *'krines'*. The *'krines'* part means *referee* and the other *'eili'* has its roots in the word *glow*. That means the word *'eilikrines'* means the purity, which comes when the referee proves its glow. It shines and its shining is proven by a referee. The referee validates its light that is the sense it brings. So God has to approve you by judging you or being an umpire to your soul. You see when something is brought to a shining light and the bright light exposes it, its purity is exposed. Its purity comes to the surface. That means your mind has to be exposed to God's grade of judgement for it to shine well enough. In your friendship with God, allow Him to prove your light. Allow Him to wash you through His word and make you pure.

The Third kind of purity

When Apostle Paul was asking us to be sincere in the book of Corinthians he was actually asking us to be good or to be pure. The word sincere here is the same as the word simplicity as shown in the word. Haplotes is the word simplicity in the Greek and is closely linked to sincere here. So Apostle Paul was admonishing us to be good as this is one of the best ways to be intimate with Him. Look at the scripture below as we start with this word sincere then we move on to haplotes when we've describe simplicity:

1 Cor.5: 8
"Therefore let us keep the feast, not with old leaven, nor with the leaven of malice and wickedness, but with the unleavened bread of sincerity and truth."

Intimacy

When you see the word 'leaven' you know we are talking about being bad. Yeasts can be found everywhere in nature, especially on plants and fruits. After fruits fall off the tree, fruits become rotten through the activity of moulds, which form alcohol and carbon dioxide from the sugars in it. Sometimes drunk animals appear in the news because they have eaten these spoiled fruits. Funny, but true. So yeast is bad according to the word here. It carries rotten components so Apostle Paul says:

1 Cor.5: 8 *"Therefore let us keep the feast, not with old leaven, nor with the leaven of malice and wickedness, but with the unleavened bread of sincerity and truth."*

So the above verse shows us that Apostle Paul is talking about purity because leaven in the bread defiles it. Remember this is the same thing the Lord Jesus Himself told his disciples in Matthew 16 vs. 16, He says:

"...beware of the leaven of the Pharisees..."
Here he was telling them to run away from being defiled. The Lord wanted his disciples to keep goodness that will not be defiled. Jesus was telling them to be sincere, to be pure, and to be upright. Without this He knew there was no way we were going to become intimate with Him. There was no way they were going to be His best friends. So when you want to grow closer to God by romancing His heart you ought to become sincere. That is what you do. You become an upright person. God is faithful; He desires for us to draw nigh to Him as He draws nigh to us.

Intimacy

But what is a sincere person? A sincere person is mainly seen by what comes out of their mouth. A sincere person is a simple person in the sense of simplicity. Notice that the Pharisees would speak volumes and the Lord told His disciples to be aware of what the words were. Did they give a sense of simplicity in the speaker or was there a different feel to their words. Were they saying one thing and doing another? This attitude is seen by the word *haplotes*. In other words he was saying the leaven was their words, in a way telling his own disciples that if they wanted to run away from those words they need to care about what enters into their ears: He was in a way saying;

"...Be careful what you hear..."

What the Pharisees said was the leaven so the sign of a good person is also measured by what comes out of their mouth. A good man is a man of few words. Intimacy is all about maintaining a life that is separated. A person who is intimate with God is a person who knows no gossip or tolerates it. If you know anyone who is prone to gossip, that is a big sign they are far from being intimate with God. They do not have a friendship with God.

There is a woman I used to know who knew everything about anyone. She was in people's business all the time. She even got the nickname BBC by people in the community. I later heard that her husband had divorced the woman as he had had enough of her meddling in other people's affairs. She was so far from God that she had become a gossiper by nature.

Good (katharos) people are people who can have haplotes (sincerity). The heart is good so the mind will also be good if the heart controls it. A good person may not come across as good sometimes but they mean what they say. There is no malice in their heart.

However there are people who will always claim to be good. Some will claim to be very sincere but their sincerity is sincerely wrong! It's the same concept with people who go on and on saying they are spiritually mature when they aren't. They do not realize that when you do become 'mature' spiritually, you actually realize that there is a whole lot of knowledge about the things of God that you did not know. It's as if the more you grow, the more you realize that there is so much more about God at each level of growth.

You see goodness or purity is not something you just claim you have. It is something with evidence to it. Something that carries proof and people can actually confirm the fact that you are a good and pure person. Good people are contagious. They have a lifestyle built on a well-cultivated intimate relationship with God. You sit around them long enough they will either bore you to death or push you into being good friends with God. That is their nature. They are just good and the light in them is very bright that the darkness in their enemies cannot stand. It will flee away. These people are full of light.

I recall a time when I started going to University. On the very first day before having known anyone, one Caribbean lady came to where I was and said to me "I know you are a

Christian, can I sit with you?" I was a little surprised at how she knew this, as I had never met this person before. She went on to say that there was just something about me that was sincere and kind and that's how she figured that I was a believer. The irony of the issue is that she wasn't even a Christian herself. She had last stepped foot in a church when one of her relatives died and it had been fifteen years to that date. It was not like I had a badge that announced my love of Christ. There was no physical sign but there was goodness upon me that was evident to others. It was the aura of someone who is in love with Christ. An aura of intimacy with the one who created us. It is the purity and goodness that gets you to a level where you know He is in you and you are in Him, that you are best friends and no one can come between you.

Notice here how Apostle Paul continues in this light:
In 2 Corinthians we want to look at the different word here in chapter 11: 3

"But I fear, lest somehow, as the serpent deceive Eve by his craftiness, so your minds may be corrupted from the simplicity that is in Christ."

In the scripture above we see another thing which is really in the same league with sincerity the word simplicity is the word *'Haplotes'*. Now *'haplotes'* has a powerful meaning and it also means a type of transparency and purity. Do you know deceiving and sly people are crafty? They know how to twist and turn their words to deceive. Paul says don't be like that because that is how the serpent is. That is how the devil is. Their yes is not always a yes. You never know when they really mean yes. Because when they say yes it might actually be a no. So you are never sure with such people. You are never sure. They will not expose the truth. They are not transparent.

For example, 2 Cor. 8 vs. 2 says:

"That in a great trial of affliction the abundance of their joy and their deep poverty abounded in the riches of their liberality."

The word liberality is the same word *'haplotes'* meaning their liberality and the generosity of their spirit that comes forth from their lives. There are no two ways about it here, only what you have deposited inside you is seen in your actions. So their heart is good, their soul is good and now their actions are proving to be good. Now that is what God calls goodness. There is no lying with these guys they are really showing what they have on the inside. When you are good you don't have to swear by anything. You actions will be proof enough. That is why the bible in James 5 vs. 12 says,

"...Don't swear by the earth or by heavens..."

When you are good, your actions will do the swearing on their own. You see I have heard people promise my husband and I heaven on earth in businesses that we run and even in our ever widening ministry. We have seen this proof in many ways. In business I have been promised the earth and people swearing by their pay checks that they were not

Intimacy

going to leave us but they did. Many in our churches told pastors that they were now feeling at home in our church that they were not going to go but they did. This swearing did not do them any good because their actions were proving all this wrong. You see their promise could not substitute their bad hearts, bad soul and bad actions. They spoke but they could not act it. Do you see that this goodness is not at all as easy as people think goodness can be explained?

You see that when you are good you don't have to swear by the earth or anything else for that matter. No wonder the word says in Matthew 5 vs. 37,

"...Let your yea be a yea and your no be a no."

You don't have to swear by anything. If you apply these principles, what you say is what you mean. You mean what you say and say what you mean. That is what you do. That's it. Not trying to make everyone happy by kissing up to them. What you say is what it is, no matter people like it or not. You are a person of your word and your actions. Your 'yes' never means a 'maybe', your yes is yes, your no is no. You see there are some people who say some things and never leave out the words, "to be honest with you" or "to tell you the truth..." then you know they have been lying all along. This is one of the signs that show you a person has no sincerity. Their words cannot be trusted all the time and they know it that is why they want you to know that this time they are being honest with you. Some say, "God is my witness..." you know they might be telling you the truth at that time but that shows they do not always tell the truth. Something is very bad in them that they need to put the word God in front for them to show people that they are truthful or to validate a point. This is a sign of lack of goodness (purity) of the heart, goodness of the soul and also a lack of goodness of the actions.

You are a transparent person. With you there is no hiding. You hide nothing from people. You have great integrity and every genuine person would want you close by. Even bad people would want to do business with you.

How to flow in goodness

You see here that goodness is in threefold. There is goodness of the heart which is related to *katharos*. There is goodness of the soul which is related to the word *eilikrines*. And there is goodness in your action, which is *haplotes*. One then cannot claim that they are really good until they are good in three areas. You cannot also claim that you have an intimate relationship with God. It starts in their heart first, in their souls and ultimately in their actions or in their body. When your heart begins to be pure or good, it is the evidence of intimacy starting up. You are getting closer and closer to feeling the 'pulse of God'. You are moving at the same pace with God and you know He is your best friend come what may. That Goodness therefore is not a matter of talking, it is a 'violent' goodness that causes one to be called good and stems from way in the spirit and then in the soul and as aforementioned in the actions of the person. A good and pure person shines with an aura that speaks volumes of their relationship with God. They are sincere; they are good, kind and just generally nice people to be around because their intimacy with God is so contagious. It can spread like a virus to those who are willing to go into a deep and meaningful friendship with God. Let the virus begin!

Chapter Four

Obedience is better than sacrifice

The book of 1 Samuel 15 vs. 22 says:
"...**Behold, to obey is better than sacrifice and to hearken than the fat of rams**"

If you look at the preceding passage of this scripture, you will be amazed at some principles that God has since established that stand to this day. Saul had been commanded to kill ALL the Amalekites AND their cattle. Instead of doing so he preserved the king and told his people to take the best of the oxen and of the sheep. When called to account for this he declared that he did it with a view of offering sacrifice to God—but Samuel met him and immediately told him that it was simply rebellion. Saul was sincerely wrong by trying to do God a favor without being asked to do it.

In this book I have mentioned that I will be sharing secrets that will help you to become intimate with God. By learning these secrets, you are getting more and more acquainted with how to access the most holy place and have a relationship that is like no other with God. You will learn to romance the heart of God and gain access into His secrets, into what He really means to you. Obeying the voice of God is better than any 'sacrifice' you may bring in the house of God. There is no way God is going to draw nigh to us if we have no tendency to obey him. He would rather we listen to His instructions than make Him happy. We automatically make Him happy if we follow His commands.

Now lets focus on the passage again. We are told that to listen to His instructions with an attentive ear is better than to bring the fat of rams and lay them upon the altar. There are some people who are reading this book right now who are living in the neglect of a certain duty, command or calling. They know exactly what they should be doing and may even have had it confirmed or even warned by a man or woman of God yet they still neglect it. Their minds have been enlightened in that area yet they still choose not to follow. If you are failing to keep the least of one of Christ's commands, be disobedient no longer. This is one of the reasons why most believers are not friends of God. They go to church and are tongue talking but still remain inanimate when it comes to intimacy with God.

There are some so called believers who are living on evil trade. They know that their means of acquiring money leave a lot to be desired. Their conscience has even shouted time and time again to "get out of it!" yet they continue in their folly.

There is a man who visited our church once a few years ago. On that occasion he came to me for prayer after the service was finished and said; "I have a loan that I have applied for and I just need you to pray for me so everything can go through fine". At first it seemed like a normal request anyone would give until I the Lord spoke to me in detail about this '. I told him what the Lord had told me that the loan was not even in his own name. He had used a bogus name to apply for the loan and it turned out that this was actually his full time job. He would go around different banks across the country applying for loans under different names. I told him God would never bless such a trade what foolishness!

The man had gone for so long in his thievery that even his conscience was now seared with a hot iron. He had the audacity to come for prayer for such a thing. No matter what sacrifice he had laid on the altar of God, God was not pleased with it. It is simply rebellion to try and overlook things that are wrongly done and still 'praise' God after disobeying. God is not interested in our fat rams. He is more interested in us listening to what He says and following it. He knows that if we are ever going to have an intimate friendship with Him, we need to first learn to follow His commands.

There are some people who are in churches that they know are not following the statutes of God yet they remain there. They know that they should not be tolerating half the things that go on in the church yet they stay there because they have a 'position'. They have figured that if they leave, they will not have any position in another church. Your 'position' is the fat of rams and to obey God is better than anything else in this world.

Notice in the New Testament there is a lot of emphasis on the importance of obeying the will of God. The Lord Jesus Christ Himself was obedient to the heavenly father. Look at the book of Hebrews:

Hebrews 5 vs. 8-9
Though he as a Son, yet learned he obedience by the things which he suffered; and having been made perfect, he became unto all them that obey him the author of eternal salvation.

The Lord Jesus Christ Himself had to obey the will of the Father. You see God will never ask us to do what He knows is unachievable. He did it and if he did it, we can too.
To the Philippians, Paul said of Christ,

Philippians 2:8
And being found in fashion as a man, he humbled himself, becoming obedient even unto death, yea the death of the cross.

Jesus was obedient till the day he died. There was not a day that he rebelled or disobeyed what he had been instructed to do.

There was a man who once came to my husband saying he had an important question to ask. He said; "Prophet are we allowed to take part in playing the lottery if you have a dream of the winning numbers? Because I have an idea of taking part and if I win, I will use the money to build a children's home". You see this person did not really intend to build a children's home only. He simply looked for a good excuse to gamble and also get something out of it. My husband then said "Do you mean you have a dream and someone comes and says 2, 4,7,32 etc? Well it's wrong it's just a game of chance it's gambling…"

Before he'd even finished speaking, the man said; "wait wait man of God can you repeat those numbers I need to write them down".

What a mess! The guy thought that the numbers prophet had just given as an example were actually prophetically inspired winning numbers for him to play the lottery with. He wanted to sacrifice something while in disobedience.

God just wants people to love and follow Him personally, not just as an outward show that is skin deep, or as devotion to earn points with Him. It's not about gaining points by sacrificing different things; it's all about relationship. God wants us to be close to Him. He wants us to learn to romance His heart and function the way He functions. He has a desire for us to know Him and gain secrets from Him. The book of Jeremiah says,

Jeremiah 33 vs. 3
Call to me and I will tell you great and unsearchable Things you did not know.

God desires intimacy. He wants us to have a genuine love and friendship that keeps us yearning for more time with Him. He wants us to have access into unsearchable things of heaven.

The Lord Jesus Christ was the ultimate sacrifice. God gave Christ so that we don't have to try and score points with Him. Because of The Lord Jesus Christ we now have the ability to walk boldly into the holy of holies and speak mysteries with God. This is the reason why you will find great men and women of God doing exploits in the name of Jesus and others do not. It is the degree of intimacy. They have now intermingled themselves so much in a deeply intimate relationship with God. They have handled the word of truth, which is His word and have lived and walked in its pages.

My husband has a prophetic office that gives him the ability to see into people's lives- where they have come from, intimate details like names addresses, the dreams they had and when things are to happen with dates and all. He just knows the secrets people, ALL because of intimacy. Yes he has an office of a Prophet but intimacy plays an important role. He has reached a level where God will even tell him football scores well before the matches are over. He knows events in places he has never heard of or imagined from hurricanes to earthquakes to famous people dying. They are such good friends him and God that He lets him in on information on who will win even a tennis match with the exact scores open to him!

One afternoon I was watching a tennis match where one of the Williams sisters was playing. You see they are the only reason I watch tennis. Halfway through the match, my husband came into the room and casually told me who was going to win and exactly how the match was going to end

Intimacy

including the exact sets. Sometimes it's a waste of time watching anything with him. He will tell you exactly how it will end before it even starts. He just has inside information about things. God will just figure that He has to tell His friend how the football match is going to go. He managed to gain access into the secrets of God. He reached a degree of intimacy that enables him to know those great and unsearchable things God spoke of in the book of Jeremiah. One famous person he told the whole church would die was Michael Jackson, the famous singer. He was even allowed by God to see the exact day and the time, including the ambulance colour and shape and what the news headlines were to say. It's like the heavens opened to him and he was shown a pre-play of the news bulletins.

He has also been used in administering complete healing of critical diseases including HIV AIDS, cancer; heart problems, diabetes and a host of many other. Intimacy can cause a lot of things. It will not make one a Prophet but it will let you in on secrets from above. Glory be to God!

Obedience respects the moment of the command
"By faith Abraham when he was called to go out into a place which he should after receive for an inheritance, obeyed; and he went out, not knowing whither he went."—Hebrews 11:8.

Hey, look at Papa Abraham! The most striking thing in this scripture passage is the fact that Abraham was called, and he obeyed there and then. There is no hint of hesitation or doubting the word of God concerning his life. He didn't

Intimacy

question God as to where he should go and how. Nowadays we have people who approach us unsure of whether God called them or not. They question their calling and those who are sure about their calling want to know the 'whens and how's'. Questions like "When should I start obeying what God told me concerning my duties in church" or "should I go to this city or that" or "should I choose this person to marry over that one". All these questions stem from uncertainty. They come from people whose lives are not intimate with God. Abraham (an Old Testament guy) was not moved by any of these things. All he had was a word and he was going to run with it the moment it was given. You have to understand that there is nothing wrong with CONFIRMING things with men or women of God especially Prophets. A Prophet will never tell you something you had not at least thought of even for a fleeting moment. They are there to confirm what God has already dropped in your spirit not to tell you what to do that you don't even have any prior knowledge of. My husband always says, "There is no greater prophecy concerning your life than the word of God written in the Bible". Hold fast to His word. When you are intimate with God, simply obey the moment of the command. It shows your respect and trust in Him and this allows you to draw nearer and nearer to Him while He inches closer to you too.

Just before we started Spirit Embassy, I recall a certain brother who was sent by God to assist us in launching the ministry. One day my husband called him first thing in the morning and told him that God had given us the word to start the ministry immediately so we were going to be starting the following Sunday. There was hesitation on the other end and then the man said, "Brother lets pray about this for at least another year and review the situation then." What? Obedience respects the moment of command! If you have a word from God run with it. The consequences that this man received as a result are so big that even today he is still struggling and Spirit Embassy through thick, thin and persecution is seeing growth at an unprecedented rate.

Look, It does not matter who says what. It can be in ministry, business, relationships and even your healing. All you need is a word and the bible tells us that,

Philippians 1 vs. 6
"...He who began a new work in you He is faithful enough to complete it..."

There is no need to analyse anything and keep praying about the same thing God has already confirmed. Sometimes you hear some people saying, "Oh I will start cleaning the church soon, I'm just still praying about it". What is there to pray about? Is there a need in the house of God? If yes then fulfil it. Has God said what you are praying about should be done? If it is in the word then yes let it be established immediately. It's as simple as that. Obedience has a time factor and that is- NOW! If you send your child to go and pour you a glass of milk and they bring the milk after six months can you still say your child obeyed you? Obedience respects the moment of command.

When Abraham was called to go out, he went out. He was in such a good friendship with God that he never doubted the word of His lover.

They were so intimately involved that Abraham now knew that he could fully trust the word of his God. There are many who are called to do different things that will benefit the work of God but the word of God says,

Matthew 22 vs. 14
"Many are called, but few are chosen."

Why? It's because others have gone beyond the borders of what society calls a 'normal' Christian life. They have gone past the outer court and into the most sacred place with God. These are the chosen ones.

Hebrews 11 vs. 8
By faith Abraham when he was called to go out into a place which he should after receive for an inheritance, obeyed; and he went out, not knowing whither he went.

Now what we do not know from this passage is how this instruction was given.

Was it through a dream, or God used an audible voice, or by a prophet who is not mentioned, we cannot tell. We have had too many instructions ourselves and I know most people would say; "If I heard the real audible voice of God giving me instructions, I will definitely follow it immediately". Listen to what Apostle Peter says,

2 Peter 1 vs. 18
"And this voice which came from heaven we heard, when we were with him in the holy mount"

This is amazing. The man heard an audible voice from God Himself coming from heaven. How many yearn for such a moment? But more to my amazement is the fact that the Apostle adds in the next verse,

2 Peter 1 vs. 19,20
We also have a *more sure word of prophecy*; whereunto ye do well that ye take heed...knowing this first, that no prophecy of the *scripture* is of any private interpretation

The man is saying the word we have in the bible is actually better than the audible voice coming from heaven. He calls it a "more sure word of prophecy". Why is this so? It's because an audible voice may not belong to God. You might hear it, but was it really God? You may even start questioning yourself on whether you imagined it or not. It requires someone who is incredibly intimate with God to discern that it is the voice of God in the first place. When it comes to the logos, the written word of God, we all believe that it is God breathed. We all know that everything in the word is inspired by the Holy Spirit otherwise we are not believers. The word is already written that we are all called to,

Acts 1 vs. 8
"...preach the gospel to the ends of the world"

What audible voice do you now need for you to know that you should spread the gospel? Run with the gospel immediately. The command has already been given and the time is now for it to be obeyed. How many people have disregarded letters or notices written to them by government offices instead preferring the audible version of the words? No one! We gladly receive letters from various organisations and are even happier when it's in writing, as it becomes more binding. People who conduct business deals even prefer to complete deals in writing instead of the spoken word where authenticity is questioned. If you are promised a business deal you even request that they also confirm their word in 'black and white'. God has given us a sure word of His promises in black and white. It is a surer word that there is no room to start doubting Him now.

Obedience is a lonely affair

Notice the scripture we just highlighted on the obedience of Abraham. We are told that he was separated from his kindred. I tell you it is quite difficult for someone to just up and leave those closest to him. Abraham became like a banished man. It is as if he was outlawed.

There is a big revelation here that teaches us exactly how we should live. There is no way you can grow intimate with God when you are always with Chaneyney and Ray Ray. No way.

My husband often says that the Prophetic anointing is a lonely one. In order for you to grow stronger in it, you have to live a separated life. You are not found where everyone is and you cannot be with everyone either. We spend most of our time in bible study and prayer. Whatever social life we have is only between the two of us. We are always together. Why? Obedience is a lonely affair. The anointing itself to be maintained means to be lonely. We are never among this crowd today and at this function tomorrow. Unless we are in church, we never attend 'social gatherings'. Do we love being with people? Of course, but we now understand that intimacy with God comes when you focus only on Him with very little or no distraction whatsoever. When you are separated, you begin to see yourself moving from the outer court lifestyle, into the inner court and eventually you find yourself in the most holy place. You begin to master the art of romancing the heart of God.

Abraham was such a good friend of God that he was ready to take head-on whatever was to come his way. All losses and risks that may have come as a result of obeying God- he was ready. You see these are the benefits of someone who has a friend they trust and love. We have that friend in Jesus Christ. We can trust Him even if what he commands us to do is uncertain or unpopular with other people. Look at Isaiah, he was ordered to preach naked for three years,

Isaiah 20 vs. 2
At the same time spake the Lord by Isaiah the son of Amoz, saying, Go and loose the sackcloth from off thy loins, and put off thy shoe from thy foot. And he did so, walking naked AND barefoot.

And why did God do this? It was "for a sign and wonder upon Egypt and upon Ethiopia" (verse 3).

Intimacy

Now this is a hard one. I'm imagining my husband coming to tell me,

"Honey God said I should not wear my Canalli suit to church anymore". I would probably say, "Oh okay which designer are you going for now?"

"No I don't mean it that way. I mean not wearing anything at all as in no item of clothing whatsoever for the next three years *only*"

Now at that I would be gob smacked. I might even ask him to call other "major prophets" to confirm that word. To speak to God again and really really confirm that word just in case he didn't get it right the first time. Praise God!

Like Abraham, the Prophet Isaiah did not question God on the 'morality' of what he was asking him to do. He didn't say "what are people going to think of me God no please don't do this to me". He simply obeyed. What tenacity of faith and a show of great obedience on the Prophets part. How intimate he must have been with His creator that he would trust Him to that extent. An intimate friendship cultivated by living a separated life and going deeper in the knowledge of God.

Hebrews 11 vs. 8
By faith Abraham when he was called to go out into a place which he should after receive for an inheritance, obeyed; and he went out, not knowing whither he went.

Now notice that from this scripture you learn that Abraham waived the present for the future. He stepped out by faith not looking at his present situation. It did not matter what sacrifice he had to make at that time. It did not compare with what God had laid up for him.

Papa Abraham is a good example to follow. He committed himself to God by faith. He had no one else but God from the day he left his people. He had only God as his source and because he had developed intimacy with his creator, he knew he did not have anything to worry about. He simply stepped out in faith not knowing where to go.

He was ignorant as to when to stop and when to journey on, except as the Lord God guided him hour by hour.

Obedience respects the moment of command and is a lonely thing. In the New Testament lies a perfect example of the time factor when it comes to obedience. After having been told the Macedonian vision, the followers of Apostle Paul went immediately to fulfill what they'd been told to do. Look at what it says in Acts 16 vs 9.

And a vision appeared to Paul in the night; there stood a man of Macedonia, and prayed him, saying, come over into Macedonia, and help us.

This is the vision that the Apostle saw in the night. Verse 10 says,

And after he had seen the vision, IMMEDIATLEY we endeavored to go into Macedonia, assuredly gathering

that the Lord had called us for to preach the gospel unto them.

Notice that the person who saw the vision was Apostle Paul. It was not his co-workers. All he did was see the vision and relay it to the people. The people then understanding that obedience respects the moment of command, IMMEDIATLEY started preparing to go there and then. None of them questioned the authenticity of the vision. None of them said that they needed to 'pray about it first'.

This statement is now being used so loosely that it has lost its flavor. Everyone seems to 'praying about' something in today's church. To fellowship after church- they are praying about that. To follow what the Pastor said – they are still praying about it. To have family prayers and devotions – they need to pray about it first. Some even pray about whether they should go to work or staying at home! Why don't you pray about eating? When you are called to eat, why do you not pray about it first? You see there is nothing to still pray about when you have a sure word from God. When you choose to obey God fully you will notice that friends become few, as following God is not very popular. Obedience is there and then. It's not after two hours or ten minutes or even five minutes. It's a NOW thing.

Apostle Paul simply arose from sleep, told people what God had said and they went on it right away.

My husband once told one of our Pastors to go and preach at one of our conferences in another town. He gave him a specific day to go to the place about three days before the conference was to start. The total journey time was going to be twenty –four hours. We were surprised however, to receive phone calls the following day from the people who were waiting for him saying he had not arrived at the planned time. We called his house and were told he had left a day later and he had also made a detour to go and see some of his relatives since the conference was two days away. He did not respect the moment of the command and because of that his journey was no longer covered.

First among a host of inconveniences the coach broke down in the middle of nowhere and it was so late at night that there was no one to call for help and no other vehicles were passing by to offer any help. When they finally fixed the problem a few hours later and had not driven more than an hour, the coach broke down again and this time they waited throughout the whole night before anything could be done about the problem. As if this was not enough, his phone was stolen at some point during the journey and no one could get a hold of him. Meanwhile, the conference had started where he was supposed to be preaching. We had to improvise and quickly find someone to stand in for him.

To cut the long story short, the Pastor arrived half way through the second day of the conference. Some people had already left because the man they had been told was coming to preach did not come.

You see that. All because someone decided to not follow direction, it presented a lot of calamities along the way.

When you have a man of God leading and guiding you, endeavor to follow his instructions immediately. By so doing, you become attuned to the way God works. God requires us to obey and do things immediately. By obeying a man of God, you obey God Himself. The bible tells us that,

John 5 vs. 37-38
And the Father that sent me has given proof about me himself. But you have never heard his voice. You have never seen what he looks like. The Father's teaching does not live in you. Why? Because you don't believe in the One the Father sent.

In your quest to grow intimate with God, perform self-examination and see whether you concentrate on sacrifice more than obedience or whether you obey but do not respect the exact moment the instruction is given. These are some of the principles that will draw you closer to God and Him to you. Intimacy means loving God's word and that is not just promises of good things for our lives. It's also us following instructions in his word. He says in the book of John,

John 14 vs. 15
If you love me, keep my commandments

According to God, there is no way we can claim we are intimate with Him if we do not follow His instructions immediately. One of the best ways to romance the heart of God is to keep His commandments and endeavor to fulfill them promptly.

You see intimacy is no minor thing. It is intense. It is indeed one of those gems that are concealed in the word of God just waiting to be found by those that truly love Him. In the next chapter I want to show you through scripture how love complements everything you have learnt so far.

Chapter Five

LOVE GOD, LOVE YOUR BROTHER

Love thy Neighbor - Christ's Answer to Religion

When my husband received the vision to start the ministry, it was way back when he was in primary school at the age of seven. From that time he started knowing things that would happen way before they took place. It was just amazing. When he got to the age of seventeen his remarkable gift just trebled in intensity. The Lord would show him extreme things and they would take place.

Up to the time we got married, he had gotten to a level where it was impossible for him not to know details about the future of anything he enquired of the Lord. All this is information we knew but to the public, it was not known, they thought the time he started the ministry is the time it all began. Well, they are wrong!

I remember days when people would call us on the phone and shout all sorts of abuse at us. Some would lie on us and spread all sorts of rumors all based on jealousy. It was difficult to love people like that. How could they do that when we knew we were called from way back to do what we do? Many lied, many acted like they knew us when they didn't. As you know it is the habit of little people to claim to know big people. So if people are spreading lies about you and claiming they know you when they don't – know you are big.

At the time we started the church we didn't even take tithes and offerings as a way of proving to people that we were not in it for the money. We tried to move as far away as possible from getting people to think we had started the church for money. So to hear people accusing us of lying and stealing from people was hurtful.

When the prophecies started getting fulfilled, the people changed but not for the better, they started saying we were using black magic we had bought from somewhere and they even had dates for when this supposed black magic was purchased. This gift was made manifest when my husband was seven years old, yet to them we had purchased it from somewhere best known to them. The devil was just using people to lie.
The grace of God and deep-set Intimacy is what has helped us to get to a level where we love the people who oppose the move of God taking place in our ministry.

We had to love these people even when it hurt to love them. How can you love someone who is always lying on you and changes statements every time? God told us to love them and at first we could not bring our feelings to love them and yes many told us it had nothing to do with feeling yet that was only a representation of the first part of intimacy. Deep intimacy feels what God feels that when you attain it, you would begin to love even those who are not lovable even with your feelings involved. One ought to have intimacy in order to feel for those who are not lovable.

Getting into intimacy with the Lord is something that also relies on your ability to love the people that God created. The most basic yet important nature of God is love. When we love others with unselfish love, we are taking on the nature of God and in effect loving him. We are commanded to love God and love our neighbor as our self. When we do this, we are demonstrating that we love God.
You see God wants us to 'romance' His heart. Love is the epitome of this book. How can we have an intimate relationship with God if we do not possess the most basic nature of a believer, which is love? God wants us to love what He loves, hate what He hates not because it's written but because we are in love with Him, our will changes to His will. He wants it to be so, so that our will changes not because He wants us to change them only but because there is something in Him and in us that is now knit together because of intimacy that calls for it. Being in love should be the reason why I have the ability to love my friends and enemies alike.

The Lord Jesus Christ said,

Matthew 22 vs. 37
Love the Lord your God with all your heart and with all Soul and with all your mind

After saying that he uttered words many have not yet taken into their heart. He said

"...this is the greatest command..."
Verse 38

I explained earlier how believers have been taught wrong on these Hebrew and Greek words that define love. They think God only has agape. This is ignorance gone on rampage. Other languages like Greek and even Latin have different words for love. Some of these are brotherly love, sexual love, friendship love, logical love, smothering love and divine love. English language on the other hand has only one word for love. This is exactly why people have trouble defining love. Let's take a look at two important types of love. Unless you understand the dynamics of the nature of love, it is very difficult to get to a level where God calls you lover and friend.

Philleo versus Agape

God is Agape but agape contains all the other properties of love like philleo. This is what the church does not understand. Philleo is not a different side of love but a component inside agape. Stay with me here and you will see the truth of it. The word if practiced without tradition will sort out many problems. Notice that the bible does not present God as having only agape. This is a mistake of the teachers that teach us or taught us.

God also wants us to have the philleo type of love toward Him which in the Strongest Concordance is 'to kiss as a matter of tenderness and chiefly connected to the heart more than to the head'. Philleo means to have affection for, to be a friend to. It is a fondness that comes from deep inside our hearts.

People have been told all you need is agape and that no believer has philleo towards the Lord. Well this is not true because they work together anyway because agape is the egg which has a yolk, egg white and shell. Philleo is part of agape. It is just another level of agape!

John 16 v 27 says,
"For the Father Himself loveth you, because ye have loved Me, and have believed that I came out from God."

The word 'love' there is philleo. This means affection. Do you see that the verse is telling us that God has philleo? This shows that even God possesses philleo towards his children. It is love that comes from deep within that has everything to do with feelings. Philleo love works together with all the other types of love stated in the bible to build up a believer who is intimate with God. This is what intimacy is all about. Philleo is about *feeling* the love of God and *feeling* in love with Him. It is not a decision that you make to forcefully love Him even if you don't feel like it. Philleo is the love of things we have understanding of. If you have an understanding of who God really is to you, you don't need anyone to force you to love Him. You can't help but love him. You gain an insatiable desire to romance His heart and draw closer to Him.

Agape on the other hand works similarly to philleo. They both work together. First you make a decision to understand and seek the best for others then you have good feelings towards them- you genuinely love them. This is a love based in the mind first. Feelings are also incorporated in this type of love. You can choose to show agape love by actively thinking about, and deciding how to act and feel love toward other people. Agape is the word used when the Bible talks about Christian love for one another. Agape is the mother. Philleo does not have agape but agape contains philleo. Do you get that? It is very simple but in desperation to find something we can only attribute to God our teachers have messed up a lot of revelation and we are going only on tradition yet the word proves that God has both agape and philleo.

Hebrews 13 vs. 1
"Let brotherly love continue"
Agape love is talking about our behavior towards others. You choose to love people especially those who hate you– that is agape. It's based on a decision in the mind and then you act it out and eventually have genuine good feelings towards these people. This is the way God operates. God does not just love us because He's got no choice. He loves all of us because He genuinely has good feelings towards us. He shines His light on both sinners and believers alike. The reason why He does not strike unbelievers dead on the spot is because He loves them.

God has agape and He also has philleo. They all interlink and work hand in hand. Intimacy calls for everything you have. Romancing the heart of God is chief over everything. The art of romancing God's heart gets one into the very presence of God way beyond the veil.

The word of God also says;

Matthew 22 vs. 37
Love the Lord your God with all your heart and with all Soul and with all your mind

We have a directive to love God with everything that is within us. That means we make the decision in our minds and our minds agree with our spirits and it shows in our bodies. Our feelings are also involved here. We are not acting as robots. No, no, no we are not. We are actively involved with everything in us. Notice Isaiah says

'Your GOD IS YOUR HUSBAND…'

God has to be loved like a husband, a father and all. We also should Love like God loves. He has philleo from agape. They all work together for philleo comes out of agape though it does not necessarily contain it.

When one understands this they ought to Love their enemies genuinely by recognizing that that which makes them hate you is the spirit behind which is the devil. It's not just them so feelings should also be involved in loving the enemies if one is mature in their intimacy with God because you begin to feel for them. They hate you because there is a demon behind their hating you. It's not them. So when a believer says I just love my enemies but not with my feelings all they are telling you, no matter how mature it sounds, is they do not understand the cause of why these enemies are enemies. If they understood it they would feel for them because they are lost since the devil is causing them to hate.

There are people I have met who have the worst in-laws on earth. Their in-laws act like they are first cousins with devil himself. You just feel like acting unsaved for a minute so you can break a leg or something then ask for forgiveness later. One man I spoke to told me unbelievable things his mother-in-law was doing to him. The woman was something else! She would invent all sorts of lies, fix things so they wouldn't work for him financially and she would consult witch doctors on how to destroy her son-in-laws life. Now in a case like this you can easily accept that hatred is called for. You start binding and wishing the worst case of diarrhea on her. You wish that the ground would just open and swallow her up. You start reading the stories in the Old Testament where God showed instant justice to people who had done wrong and imagine Him doing it to her.

When this man told me about the behavior of his mother-in-law, for a split second I felt like going to where she was and punching her on the nose for what she was doing to him. So I had to compose myself before answering him. When I had managed to hold myself from within (the word of God calls this temperance), I kindly told him to just love her all the same. He found this hard to do because he was thinking I was talking about philleo alone. I was talking about philleo and agape working together. You choose to love because God loves. When God says He loves sinners, He actually loves them genuinely. He does not do it because He has no choice. He sincerely loves us, His creation.

Love thy neighbor
Matthew 7:12
"Do to others what you would have them do to you"

I find this one of the best scriptures to understand our conduct when it comes to loving one another. Most of the things we do to others we would hate if the tables were turned.

If you hate people speaking against you then don't speak against them yourself. If you hate swindlers then stop swindling others it's as simple as that! If you don't like the fact that people don't understand you then seek to understand them than to be understood. The bible is very practical- simply do to others what you would have them do to you.

So what defines a neighbor? We need to know this because if we are to grow intimate with God and love what He loves, it's imperative that we know and do the same as He does. The Lord Jesus Christ says your brother is your neighbor. In other words it's any person you come into contact with. It does not matter whether they are your best friends, archenemies or simply human beings going their way in this world, they are your neighbors.

Intimacy

Matthew 22 vs.34-40 says
Hearing that Jesus had silenced the Sadducees, the Pharisees got together. One of them, an expert in the law, tested him with this question: "Teacher, which is the greatest commandment in the Law?"

Jesus replied: "'Love the Lord your God with all your heart and with all your soul and with all your mind. 'This is the first and greatest commandment. And the second is like it: 'Love your neighbor as yourself. 'All the Law and the Prophets hang on these two commandments.

These religious leaders called the Pharisees had an aim, which was to test Jesus. They were trying to catch him unaware but the Lord knew it and gave a very remarkable answer. He made the distinction between laws and this comparison in the laws prove the importance of loving your brother.

His answer stunned them and that answer comes in the form of Matthew 22 vs. 34 to 40 above.

One thing the Lord Jesus was doing here was to sum up all the law in these two statements. If we love the Lord God with all our heart, soul and mind, loving our neighbor is the natural result. Let's look at who Jesus says our neighbor is in His own words,

Matthew 5 vs.43
You have heard that it was said, 'Love your neighbor and hate your enemy.' But I tell you: Love your enemies and pray for those who persecute you.

The Lord Jesus is putting enemies as our friends. Literally he is just saying in layman terms, the person next door and the person afar off. It's one and the same thing. I should love them all the same.

If we want to love God with all our heart, soul, mind and strength, we should realize that everyone is part of His creation and God loves them so if He loves them, we need to love those He loves so intimacy can work. In fact as you saw God has put that as His top priority on the Ten Commandments.

God loves sinners but hates the sin. We should also endeavor to love sinners but hate their actions. We love our enemies because we are lovers but it does not mean we like what they do. We commonly think of neighbors as the people who live near us, but Jesus meant it to include all mankind - even our enemies! Jesus told His famous parable of the Good Samaritan to make it clear that "love your neighbor" means to love all persons, everywhere - not just those who live near us, friends and countrymen.

This is how the parable goes,

"A Jew going on a trip from Jerusalem to Jericho was attacked by bandits. They stripped him of his clothes and money, and beat him up and left him lying half dead beside the road. "By chance a Jewish priest came along; and when he saw the man lying there, he crossed to the other side of the road and passed him by. A Jewish

Temple-assistant walked over and looked at him lying there, but then went on. "But a despised Samaritan came along, and when he saw him, he felt deep pity. Kneeling beside him the Samaritan soothed his wounds with medicine and bandaged them. Then he put the man on his donkey and walked along beside him till they came to an inn, where he nursed him through the night. The next day he handed the innkeeper two twenty-dollar bills and told him to take care of the man. 'If his bill runs higher than that,' he said, 'I'll pay the difference the next time I am here.'

"Now which of these three would you say was a neighbor to the bandits' victim?" The man replied, "The one who showed him some pity." Then Jesus said, "Yes, now go and do the same."

The Jews and Samaritans had been enemies for hundreds of years. Yet, the Samaritan took pity on the poor man who had been robbed and beaten. He gave freely of both his time and his money to help this Jewish man who was not only a stranger, but also an enemy from a foreign country. He ceased to care about the all else and just focused on a human being who had a need and he could furnish that need. He was simply doing what he would expect someone else to do for him. In His parable of the Good Samaritan, Jesus challenges us to **"Go and do the same."**

Jesus goes on to reinforce the rule of love to even our enemies! He says in Matthew 5 vs. 43-48

Intimacy

"There is a saying, 'Love your friends and hate your enemies.' But I say: Love your enemies! Pray for those who persecute you! In that way you will be *acting as true sons of your Father in heaven*. For he gives his sunlight to both the evil and the good, and sends rain on the just and on the unjust too. If you love only those who love you, what good is that? Even scoundrels do that much. If you are friendly only to your friends, how are you different from anyone else? Even the heathen do that. *But you are to be perfect, even as your Father in heaven is perfect.*

Notice on the first part of the scripture the Lord Jesus Christ Himself is instructing us to love our enemies SO THAT we act as true sons of our father in heaven. See that? We cannot gain intimacy if we cannot get ourselves to love those who hate us. The object of intimacy is to know God better and act the same way He acts, think the same way God would think. True sons and daughters of God do what the Father does.

Love what God loves, hate what he hates!

"Love thy neighbor" is not as hard as it looks on the surface. It simply means respecting others and regarding their needs and desires as highly as we regard our own. Keeping this commandment, however, is likely to require the supernatural assistance only God, through Christ, can provide. How can we learn to love the womanizing guy next door with the barking dog, run down car, unkempt dreadlocks and loud monotonous music especially when we don't even like him?

115

The secret is to recognize that your neighbor, whether it's the guy next door, the checker at the local grocery store, or the annoying Sunday school teacher at church, is someone as worthy of God's love as you and I.

The moment you become intimate with God, you begin to see how easy it is to love your enemies. If you love ALL your neighbors - friends and enemies alike, they begin to see the nature of Christ in you. Take a look at the scripture again,

Matthew 7:12
"Do to others what you would have them do to you"

This scripture sums up Jesus' ethical teachings in one short sentence. If we wish to be loved, we must give love. If we wish to be respected, we must respect all persons - even those we dislike. If we wish to be forgiven, we must also forgive. If we wish others to speak kindly of us, we must speak kindly of them and avoid gossip. If we want strong, talk-of-the-town marriages, we must be loyal and faithful to our spouses. If we wish to be fulfilled in our lives, we must share generously with others. If we wish to reap the rewards of our Heavenly Father's love, we must truly love all His people. If we pray for God to have mercy on us, then we need to show others mercy. If we want God to be close to us we must hold fast to the things He loves and hate the things He hates.

One of the secrets to romancing the heart of God in order to gain intimacy is to treat others, as you would want to be treated. It's as simple as that. Love everyone the way God loves them. See them with the same eyes God uses to look at people. If you love God, you will love your brother.

In the following chapter I want to share with you a profound teaching that will showcase certain attributes of the glory of God that will sum up the principles we need to learn how to romance the heart of God.

Chapter Six

Glory of God

Exodus 34:6.
"And the Lord passed before him and proclaimed, "The Lord, the Lord God, merciful and gracious, longsuffering, and abounding in goodness and truth..."

The glory of God is like a jigsaw puzzle that comes together when fitted with other pieces. It is like a beautiful mosaic that you can only appreciate if you see the full picture. It's complicated yet simple. If you have an intimate friendship with God, you begin to realize that there is so much more to Him than meets the eye. You just keep falling deeper and deeper in love with Him as you get to know Him better. The object of learning about the glory of God is for us to see how God operates and apply that to our own lives so we can be more like Him. In the process, we draw closer to God and become good friends with Him, if God is merciful, gracious, longsuffering and abounding in goodness and truth then so should we have those same attributes.

Glory is a substance. It is the tangible expression of God's presence. The glory of God is a substance that manifests in the natural realm. Although it is a spiritual substance, it can manifest in the natural realm.

Intimacy

No one has ever tried to hold steam in their fist unless they were in a lunatic asylum. It is only when the steam changes form and becomes liquid that it becomes tangible. This is exactly the same way the glory of God works. At first it will be invisible in the spirit realm but there are times when God changes the form of that invisible glory upon a person or in church. God can cause the air we breathe to solidify into a different form to make it tangible.

I want you to take a look at this passage,

Exodus 3 vs. 1
Now Moses kept the flock of Jethro his father in law, the priest of Midian: and he led the flock to the backside of the desert, and came to the mountain of God, even to Horeb. And the angel of the LORD appeared unto him in a flame of fire out of the midst of a bush: and he looked, and, behold, the bush burned with fire, and the bush was not consumed. And Moses said, I will now turn aside, and see this great sight, why the bush is not burnt.

See that? This is a clear analogy of the manifestation of the glory of God. The presence of God was tangible. The bush was actually burning but the fire did not consume it.

There have been times in Spirit Embassy when we have witnessed the manifestation of God's glory. The moment you enter any one of our church buildings, you can feel a tangible expression of this glory. The moment you walk away from such a place you can actually feel that it has lifted. The glory of God has an ability to hover over an object, over a place or a person.

Intimacy

Let us look at this passage of scripture. Moses had just seen the glory of God in the book of Exodus.

Exodus 34 vs. 29
Now it was so, when Moses came down from Mount Sinai (and the two tablets of the Testimony were in Moses' hand when he came down from the mountain). That Moses did not know that the skin of his face shone while he talked with Him. So when Aaron and all the children of Israel saw Moses, behold, the skin of his face shone, and they were afraid to come near him.

See God's glory can come on a physical object like it did on the burning bush. It can also be made manifest on a human being like it did with Moses. His face shone after the presence of God came upon him. Nothing natural caused it. Moses had simply been exposed to the glory of God.

One Saturday afternoon we were at one of our church buildings in England and my husband was teaching a few people about how the word of God speaks of us doing exploits. Daniel says it this way,

Daniel 11 vs.32
"...the people that do know their God shall be strong, and do exploits".

As he began to elaborate on this, the glory of God hit that place so hard that even as he spoke, he began to levitate off of the ground. Everyone present was utterly amazed but not as much as my husband! He often talks about this incident saying that he acted cool as it was happening yet inside he was spinning with a mixture of shock, joy and amazement! This was a clear demonstration of the glory of God made manifest.

Stay with me, as you will begin to see how this relates to you growing to a level where you and God are intimate. The glory of God can do so much to transform our lives. When you focus on God's glory, when you seek His glory, when you hunger for His glory, when you sit in the glory of His presence, a transformation takes place in your life. You are transformed to such an extraordinary level that people will be amazed at your level of intimacy with God.

To understand how exactly that transformation takes place in your life, you need to see the breakdown of God's glory in order to grow intimate with Him.

Abraham cried out to God wanting to see His glory. He said;

Exodus 33 vs. 18
"...show me your glory."

Bear in mind that when Moses said to the Lord, "Please show me your glory." He was so hungry for a close relationship with God that he said, "God please show me your glory." Then God answered him in chapter 34:5

"Now the Lord descended in the cloud and stood with him there and proclaimed the name of the Lord. And the Lord passed before him and proclaimed, "The Lord God,

merciful and gracious, longsuffering, and abounding in goodness and truth..."

Now, notice how God describes the manifestation of His glory that He was about to reveal to Moses. Let's take a look at the first description it says,

"The Lord, the Lord God, merciful..."

The merciful God

If you look at the scripture the first word out of five attributes God uses to describe His glory is 'merciful'. The Hebrew word for this is **'rachum'** which means to be full of compassion. In the book of Chapter 136 vs. 1 resides an amazing emphasis on the mercy that abounds in God, it says,

Psalms 136 vs. 1
"...His mercies endure forever"

These same words echo throughout the entire chapter a further 26 times in total. This is one of the most comprehensive statements written in the bible pertaining to the nature of God. As lovers of God, we have the reassurance that the one we are in love with is merciful. He forgives us our sin and his mercy never runs dry. It endures forever. What a God we serve! He goes past our failures to the point of our need. It's a pleasure to romance the heart of a lover who is merciful and compassionate about us. The word of God goes on to say

Lamentations 3 vs. 22- 23.
The Lord's mercies ... are new every morning.

Why does the Lord say He is merciful every morning? Ever wondered why the emphasis is on 'morning' and not on any other time of the day? It looks to me as though that scripture should have said, "Thy mercies are new every evening." People sin left right and center during the day. They indulge in gossip, in adultery and in persecuting men and women of God and all sorts of other unthinkable evil. It seems more logical for God to renew His mercy every evening after we have committed all these crimes yet he chooses to do so in the morning. Why? Because we are sinners while we are sleeping too! Whether we are awake or not, we remain sinners in His sight.

However, never continue in sin relying on this notion that "God will forgive me anyway, He is a merciful God". The bible puts it this way,

Romans 6 vs. 1
What shall we say then? Shall we continue in sin, that grace may abound? GOD FORBID!

Though He is a God full of mercy, we should not take advantage of that fact and continue doing our wrongful deeds.

After Moses asked to see God's glory, He was quite obliged. He did not shout at Moses for asking such a thing. Moses was a good friend of God's you see. They had become so close that Moses could look at himself and know that whatever he asked of the Lord could actually be granted him.

Verse 11 of Exodus chapter 33, we are told this fact quite plainly;

And the LORD spake unto Moses face to face, as a man speaketh unto his friend

There is no doubt how close these two were. Moses had managed to romance the heart of God so well that he was in on all the secrets. He had gained access into the nature of God and His characteristics so much that they spoke like a man would to his friend. You know when you speak to a true friend you have no insecurities, you do not pretend to be someone you are not, you just enjoy being around them and you can talk for hours on end and start again the next day.

Now imagine this type of friendship with God. If we have carnal friendships that we enjoy so much, what more a close friendship with God, who does not lie, does not gossip, is not jealous of me, is not looking to steal my husband or wife, is only concerned about my prosperity and has my best interests at heart? A friend who looks at me and sees me as if I am the only one who exists on this earth, who is closer to me than I am to myself, who when I face persecution reassures me that the battle is not mine but His to take over, one who never sleeps but whose job is to just look out for me? Oh what a friend we have in the Lord Jesus! He is more than life to me! Oh when I think about how good God has

Intimacy

been such a good and faithful friend to us, I get goose bumps all over me!

We have looked at mercy as how God shows it to us. Now I need to show you why it is mandatory for you to apply this same mercy on others. Forgiveness helps you more than it does the person you have forgiven.

Be merciful and enter into part of the glory of God

There was a certain couple that attended our church a few years ago. Now this couple decided to leave the church after a short while and went about the city slandering my husband and I. We had done nothing or said nothing wrong to them as far as we knew but what we got was a tirade of persecution. Some people even left the church as a result of the lies they went about spreading. After a while they fell into a serious problem and God fixed it in such a way that we were the only people who were able to help them come out of it. Despite everything they had said about us, we drove to their place offered to help and managed to fix the problem. You see these people did not deserve to be helped. After everything wrong they did to us, they deserved judgment and wrath but instead they got a merciful hand of help. God has been merciful to us therefore we learnt to be merciful to others.

Now look at Exodus 34 again it says;

Exodus 34:6.
"And the Lord passed before him and proclaimed, "The Lord, the Lord God, merciful and gracious, longsuffering, and abounding in goodness and truth…"

This was the glory of God being made manifest. God mentioned five attributes of that same glory, which are merciful, gracious, longsuffering, abounding in goodness and truth. His encounter with Moses revealed all these attributes that make up His glory. For you to have a friendship with God that others can emulate, you need to grow in all the five attributes of God's glory

If you manage to grow in mercy, you will grow in God's glory and ultimately have a close intimate relationship with Him. Mercy is to withhold judgment. To be merciful is not to always condemn people but to pardon them for the wrongful things they do.

If a person does something that is obviously wrong, he deserves to be punished for his misdeeds. But mercy shows clemency and withholds judgment even though the person really deserved to be punished greatly. If you want to grow closer to God and live in His glory, you need to grow in this attribute.

The Lord Jesus said,

Blessed are the merciful for they shall receive mercy.

Notice the desire that God has for us to have mercy on others. He promises there is something in it for us too in an effort to make us grow in mercy.

The word of God also says,

Therefore be merciful just as your Father also is merciful

It is Papa God's nature to be merciful. We are born of Him therefore mercy should be easy for us to do.

I met a sister once who told me about how her husband had run off to be with another woman. He left her 'high and dry' with no money and three children to take care of on her own. Bailiffs with court orders of unpaid debts came to the house and took all the furniture save for a few items that were of little or no value. Her husband was nowhere to be found, he had changed his number.

No one knew where he was except for a few of his friends who would occasionally inform her that they had spotted him in different locations with this other woman. She was in a dark place but the Lord is an ever-present help in times of despair. Slowly she began to recover financially and emotionally with the support of brethren in the church.

The time came after a few years that she heard that her husband was extremely ill and had been hospitalized. She wasted no time and went to be with him on his sick bed. And as you would imagine, the girlfriend was nowhere to be seen. This sister nursed and prayed her husband back to health. As soon as he recovered he went back home to be with his family. They are now a strong family unit and serve extremely well in their church. What a remarkable show of mercy. The man deserved to be tied to a tree and beaten very well but instead what he got was mercy. It placed their lives on a different course and changed them forever.

Mercy is a strange thing indeed. How does one forgive such actions? The things of God do not make sense, they make faith!

Look at Mathew 7 vs. 1 and 2,

Judge not, that you may not judge. For with what judgment you judge, you will be judged, and with the measure you use, it will be measured back to you.

Notice that this scripture does not pertain to finances. It pertains to judging others. A day is coming when we will require mercy from God and that is the Day of Judgment. If we sow mercy, we will also receive mercy. Right now is a good time to start.

Wherever there is no forgiveness, there is no glory. Wherever there is no mercy, there is no glory. The fastest way to remove God's glory out of a place so that God does not like to manifest is an atmosphere of strife and unforgiveness. But the fastest way to get God's mercy and God's glory into a place is when people grow in God's mercy. People grow to accept one another. People grow with the ability to forgive to forget, to bless and altogether to exalt the mercy of God. One of the easiest ways to stop God's anointing and glory is when people's hearts are hardened and they withhold mercy from each other.

Now I want to share with you the second attribute of Gods glory and that is grace.

The Grace of God

Exodus 34 vs. 6
"And the Lord passed before him and proclaimed, "The Lord, the Lord God, merciful and gracious…"
Grace is an often talked about word but seldom fully understood. Grace is God's unmerited favor. Grace is God doing good for us that we do not deserve. In the Bible, grace and mercy are like two heads of the same coin. Mercy is God withholding judgment or evil that I deserve; grace is God giving me blessings or good that I do not deserve. Because of God's mercy, I do not receive the judgment of God against my sins; because of God's grace, I receive eternal life and a promise of heaven though I do not deserve them.

Grace is like a person who is caught robbing a bank. But instead of being charged and being thrown into prison, the robber is let off. Not only is he let off; he is also given a mansion and two cars. That is the mathematics of grace. It does not make sense because it is grace – it is not meant to.

However, like mercy the bible tells us

"Not to continue in sin so that grace may abound."

Intimacy

When we talk about the grace of God, It is not just about people finding and seeking God; it is rather God revealing Himself. The only way you can grow in God is by His grace. The grace of God is God's revelation of Himself to us. As He reveals we receive. And if we are faithful to His word and grow intimate with Him, He will reveal more.

My husband always speaks of how it is the grace of God that has catapulted him to where he is today. He says it is not about clever decisions he made or clever strategies he has implemented for the ministry to grow as much as it has –it's all God and not him. For him to be sought after by Prime Ministers and great men is just grace.

In the Old Testament, grace is finding a position with God and reaching into the depths of God. Despite the fact that God is holy, almighty, awesome, majestic, all-powerful, radiant in all His marvelous shining glory, Moses could still approach God. He was at a level where he was able to communicate with God as unto men. How is that possible? Moses found grace in the eyes of God. God bestowed His grace upon Moses to approach Him.

In the old covenant, everyone whom God showed grace made an effort. They had to earn it. Everyone in the old covenant whom God revealed his glory has made an effort somehow. It is not that their efforts scored points with God but their efforts were the signs for their hunger for God and this is what God looks for. Those who hunger for God will find God. Those who do not hunger for God will not find Him. Before Noah found grace in the eyes of God, it is written how Noah was obedient to the Lord. He carried out instructions immediately and did not hesitate in obeying.

Daniel had to be obedient first before he could receive God's grace. You do not receive God's grace and then become obedient. You are obedient first and then you receive more. Obedience is better than sacrifice – these are just principles set in the word that will not change. God has a standard procedure to impart grace. He looks at us and seeks to impart more grace. He looks at whether we are making an effort to have a deeper relationship with Him.

See God reveals Himself in portions. We cannot fully know Him unless He reveals Himself to us. He is only willing to reveal Himself to someone who remains obedient in His word. You will begin to see the glory of God as it begins to change your life for the best. Grace in the old covenant was originally just a position but now, it is a substance imparted to our spirit. As we grow from glory to glory, more substance of God's power is imparted into our spirit man and we grow in His grace.

Longsuffering

After Moses asked, "Lord, show me your glory," the Lord appeared to him in Exodus 34: 6

And the Lord passed before him and proclaimed, "The Lord, the Lord God, merciful and gracious, longsuffering, and abounding in goodness and truth."

Intimacy

I want us to take a look at the word longsuffering and how it helps us to understand the glory of God. The glory contains five attributes of His nature and we have to have the same attributes in order for us to be with Him as friends. Longsuffering derives from a Hebrew word *erakhap,* which is a combination of two words, the word *slow* and the word *anger*.

Notice the meaning of longsuffering here is Hebrew thus different to 'longsuffering' spoken of by Apostle Paul in the book of Galatians chapter five which is the Greek word **makrothumia**. So, what God is saying about His longsuffering is that He is slow to anger. He is slow to exercise His wrath. So longsuffering brings to mind tolerance. Long suffering speaks about tolerance. God tolerates our weaknesses, our sins, our failings and disobedience. God has tremendous tolerance that we should emulate. We realize that God's patience outlasts us. God's ability to put up with us outlasts our ability to put up with others. So longsuffering is the ability to tolerate, to remain the same in spite and despite of all that may come. It is a tremendous ability that is rare to find among believers today.

I have met people who are always impatient with others. They do not tolerate the slightest mistake. They forget how much God has tolerated their mistakes over the years. We should strive to do unto others, as we would have them do to us. The book of Matthew,

Matthew 7:12
"Do to others what you would have them do to you"

They are in hot haste to see all things accomplished before the sun goes down. Most of the things are not necessary to even accomplish on the day but they are just not patient. We are staggered when the Master tells us to forgive seventy times seven. When he forgives unto seventy times seven, and still waits, and still holds back his thunders, we are amazed, because our mind is not in harmony with the mind of the Infinitely-patient God. He can easily open up the ground to swallow us when we do wrong but he still holds back and gives us a chance.

Your duty as a believer is to strive to be like Christ. If God is slow to anger then so should you. If he tolerates every sin you commit then you can forgive and give others a chance too. Note that by so saying, God does not condone sin, no. He is simply a God of second chances. What He sees is a heart that is striving to change not a hardened one. The bible says

Psalm 66:18
"If I regard sin in my heart, the Lord will not hear me"

If you continue in sin God ceases to hear you when you pray. He tolerates those that He sees have a heart to change, a repentant spirit rather than someone who regards sin and does nothing about it. He will not listen to our prayers as stated in the above scripture.

The object of learning about the glory of God is for us to see how God operates and apply that to our own lives so we can be more like Him. In the process, we draw closer to God and become good friends with Him. We gain intimacy and access into the secrets of God, which He desires to share with us.

If we go by the Hebrew word *erakhap*, slow to anger then the opposite of longsuffering is quick to anger. That's the actual Hebrew word – it is slow to anger. The opposite of that will be very quick to anger and quick to react.

I know people, men and women alike, who before they even hear the end of a story, or the other side of it they are blowing a fuse. They decide a matter by only hearing one side to an issue. The Bible describes such people this way,

"Only a fool decides a matter after hearing one side"

Our God is a God of second, third, fourth etc. chances. He does not condone sin in us but He is patient enough when He sees that our hearts are contrite. We are willing to be taught and turn away from our sin.

So we realize that God is slow to anger. So should we. Whatever we would like from God's nature, we should adopt and act likewise.

Goodness of God

"The Lord, the Lord, God, merciful and gracious, longsuffering, and abounding in goodness…"

Intimacy

The fourth attribute of God's glory is goodness. The glory of God is vital if we are to gain intimacy with the love of our life. It allows us to have that closeness we desire to have with God. We need to know what the glory of God consists of if a meaningful relationship is to be achieved with God.

The scripture in the book of Exodus which I have been using as the main reference says,

Exodus 33 vs. 19
"And the LORD said, I will cause ALL MY GOODNESS to pass in front of you, and I will proclaim my name, the LORD, in your presence..."

Did you see that? God summarizes all the five ingredients into one general word *goodness.* The way he speaks of goodness is as if it was a substance. Something tangible. He says "I will make all my goodness pass before you".

Goodness is an attribute of God. When He speaks about goodness it is about substance and attitude combined. It is different to saying someone is kind. Goodness is tangible. Psalm 23 says,

"Surely goodness and mercy shall follow me."

How can an attitude follow me? If there is any attitude following me, it should be my attitude. It should be in me, not outside following me. But there is something following us.

Surely, goodness and mercy is following me all the days of our life. And I will dwell in the house of the Lord forever.

There are benefits of being a good man.

Here is why, take a look at **Psalms. 37 vs. 23-24**

The steps of a good man are ordered by the Lord and He delights in his ways. Though he fall, he shall not be utterly cast down.

Do you see that? A good friend of God's may make mistakes and fall, yet the Lord will raise him up again. But if you are a bad man and you fall, you are not getting up. Goodness props you up in troubled times. If you understand goodness and apply it in your life, you become a good person in substance and attitude.

There is something else about goodness that preserves us. Once it gets a hold of you, it has the power to preserve you. It preserves you in imperfection. It preserves you when you make mistakes. It preserves you when you fall. So, it is a powerful attribute.

If we look at Abraham in the bible, he was a good man but he did stumble and fall. He lied that Sarah was his sister to King Abimelech.

Genesis 12 vs. 11
When he was about to enter Egypt, he said to Sarai his wife, I know that you are a woman beautiful in appearance, and

when the Egyptians see you, they will say, this is his wife. Then they will kill me, but they will let you live. Say you are my sister, that it may go well with me because of you, and that my life may be spared for your sake

Abraham told a half-truth. People call it a white lie. It is incomplete information that gets the hearer to a wrong conclusion. It is true that Sarah is Abraham's half sister. But that is half the truth. Abimelech concluded that therefore Sarah is not Abraham's wife if she were his sister. Now look at how God came to the defense of this lie,

"Restore the man's wife for he is a prophet."

God had just defended a liar. He was defending a man who has fallen. Why? because he was a good man.

Psalm 37:23-24
The steps of a good man are ordered by the Lord. And He delights in his way. Though he fall, he shall not be utterly cast down; for the Lord upholds him with His hand.

Now when you fall you pay a price for it. You set certain wheels in motion that you may not be able to stop. I am not saying you can get away with sinning but the fact of the matter is you can be restored.

If you are a habitual liar then that's a different matter. That simply means that you are not good. You have no intimacy with God otherwise you wouldn't continue to do it. I was seeing that there were other people who were now feeling elated that they were off the hook because of goodness. Not so. Continue in sin – the wrath of God will be upon you.

If you constantly repeat failures and sins you become an evil person. No one has a license to sin. What I am teaching you is for you to understand the mercy and goodness of God and how these attributes work in your life promoting intimacy. We are not Islands that stand-alone never requiring mercy and goodness of God. We cannot live without Him. If a good person falls he or she has the ability to rise up. Take a look at the book of Proverbs,

Proverbs 24 vs. 16
For a just [man] falleth seven times, and riseth up again: but the wicked shall fall into misfortune.

There are some people who are reading this book who fall from time to time. Some dare not face others when they make a mistake. They stop attending church services and figure they are able to sort themselves out at home. Since we started the ministry, we have heard time and time again different people saying they will start coming to church once they have 'sorted things out' on their own. There is no way you can sort yourself out without God. It is only if you are good that He helps you to pick yourself up. You cannot do it alone.

A good man recognizes and admits if he has sinned. Apostle Paul admitted the wrong he had done. See this is what proves whether you are a good person or not. Recognize and acknowledge the sin in your life and your need for a savior.

Notice when the world was created. God made all things and stepped back and said that it was good. When he made us he said 'it was good'. Everything that God gave is because He is good. All of creation is summarized by the word *good*. That expresses an attribute of goodness. Goodness and being good is not just refraining from evil. When we say, "I am good to you," or, "He is a good man," we should not use it in reference to just somebody who stays away from evil.

When the world measures goodness, it talks of people who just don't to bad things. The world does not add the spiritual dimension. Goodness has the ability to do something that improves you. It is not just the ability to stay away from bad things. It makes you happy.

Goodness seeks to improve not only your self but others too. A good person seeks to make others feel comfortable all the time and they normally fuss over people to make sure they are okay.

Spiritual blessings, mental blessings and physical blessings are all categorized as God's goodness. So when you have a financial blessing, it came from God's goodness.
I always speak of how good God has been to my family. He has met every promise He told us concerning our lives so far. The material wealth we have is a result of God's goodness. He has been and continues to be so good to us. He has not only been good in the material things, we are also blessed with knowledge of the things of the Spirit, health and joy. You are alive today because of the goodness of God.

How to get into goodness

So there are two areas of goodness that you need to learn in order to grow in this area. As you grow in goodness, you are growing in intimacy; you begin to develop an intimate friendship with God, which is the purpose of this book.

The first area of goodness is attitude and the other area is substance. A character of goodness takes a person who is meek and has a teachable spirit. It's a process of learning. I want to show you how to tap into the goodness of God. First lets take a look at Psalm 23.

Psalm 23 vs. 1-6
The Lord is my shepherd; I shall not want.
He maketh me to lie down in green pastures:
he leadeth me beside the still waters.
He restoreth my soul: he leadeth me in the
paths of righteousness for his name's sake.
Yea, though I walk through the valley of the
shadow of death, I will fear no evil: for thou art
with me; thy rod and thy staff they comfort me.
thou preparest a table before me in the presence
of mine enemies: thou anointest my head with
oil; my cup runneth over. Surely goodness and
mercy shall follow me all the days of my life: and
I will dwell in the house of the Lord forever

Enter the shepherd's rest

Intimacy

The second verse of this chapter speaks of entering the Lord's rest. God guides us to lie down and relax in a beautifully described place. Green pastures and still waters. A calm place that is persecution free. Whosoever says anything about you or to you simply does not affect you because you are in a position of rest. It is a place of rest where no debt, no sickness, no slander and gossip gets to you. Being led beside the still waters talks about being still and just enjoying intimacy with our God. You cease from doing everything on your own and allow God to take over.

Putting something in you.

Verse three is about restoration. When you re-store a soul, you put something inside. You instill a desire to love the Lord with everything you've got. When God leads you in the paths of righteousness - you follow righteousness. You cannot be a blessing to others if you do not understand righteousness and holiness. How can you be unrighteous and be kind at the same time? It does not work. Lead a holy and righteous life; it helps restore your soul.
The valley of the shadow of death

Genesis 22
"Give me Isaac."

God asked an extremely difficult thing of Abraham. It was a test of love. That was the valley of the shadow of death. You start your business and God blesses the work of your hands. It begins to flourish and halfway through your financial breakthrough, God shows up at the premises and says

"Is this business still yours or is it mine? You hardly have time for me as you are in meeting after meeting" God will ask you and test you. The business idea itself came from God in the first place. But the valley of the shadow of death is when your Isaac dies and God gives you a new Isaac.

Tapping into the anointing or glory of God

Verse five of Psalm 23 is one of my favorite scriptures in the Bible. Though I have enemies – he still sets tables for me. He does not just set them anywhere; he does it in front of those who hate me. So that means if I don't have enemies, no tables are laid for me. So bring on the enemies – it's my gateway to prosperity! And since the anointing now runs over me, I am well dressed to face any type of warfare.

And finally, the goodness of the Lord shall indeed follow me ALL the days of my life...

Power of truth

When Moses asked God to see His glory. God did not refuse to listen. He happily obliged because He had a good friendship with His son. They were intimate and shared secrets.

Exodus 34 vs. 6
"And the Lord passed before him and proclaimed, "The Lord, the Lord God, merciful and gracious, longsuffering, and abounding in goodness and truth."

The word truth in the Hebrew rendering is *emunah*. It conveys the meaning of a life force that comes forth from Papa God Himself. Truth is a living and flowing substance that can be imparted and given in measures. It is a component that works alongside all the other attributes to give a full experience of the glory of God. It is in learning these attributes that we sum up the level of intimacy we are to have with God.

Emunah does not convey the same meaning as truth in our English language. Truth in English is associated with mental activity like comprehension, understanding and logic. When we speak of truth some immediately think of truth as just telling the truth all the time. This is what the English word *truth* conveys. But in the Hebrew rendering of truth lies a gem that adequately describes one of the attributes of God's glory. The word truth actually means ***steadfastness***.

It is God's ability to remain in one place in season and out of season. This is the very reason why the bible says,

Hebrews 13 vs. 8
"Jesus Christ is the same yesterday and today and forever".
It is the ability to remain the same. God says He is the truth.

Intimacy

John 14 vs. 6
"Jesus saith unto him, I am the way, the *truth*, and the life…"
Papa God is talking about the ability to remain immoveable in whatever circumstances and in whatever situation. Praise God! Our God is immovable. Isn't it good to serve a God you know will never change? He never sleeps nor slumbers he remains the same. His promises remain the same. The bible says it this way,

Psalm 121 vs. 4
"Behold, he that keepeth Israel shall neither slumber nor sleep".
He is steadfast. He is forever watching out for us because He does not sleep. We have security in the one we love, the one who desires a relationship with us. So in the word of God, truth in the bible implies more than knowledge. If your knowledge is shaken it is not truth. If your principles are easily removed by every wind of doctrine that comes along, it is not truth. Truth will not have sunk into your spirit.

The most surprising thing is the Bible does not speak about truth that applies *only* to mental comprehension. It does not concentrate on it that much. The word *truth* talks about your ability to remain eternal, unchangeable, and immortal.

God is the personification of truth. He is the same yesterday, today and forever. He was, He is and He is to come. He is the One who never changes from Alpha to the Omega. He is the steadfast God who is never moved- the ancient of days Praise God! He is the Great I Am, the everlasting Father, and the extraordinary strategist who has been strategizing from eternity past to eternity future.

Truth is a force. It is a powerful substance and a force. It is not just a fact. In the normal day-to-day English language, truth and lies speak about facts that are true and facts that are not. See our English usage of the word *truth* limits what the bible is trying to bring out. This attribute of God's glory emanates from God Himself. It is the life being of God. It is his nature.

When God speaks through His word, He speaks truth, which is life. Truth is more than a fact it is a life force. The Lord Jesus said,

John 8 vs.32
And ye shall know the truth, and the truth shall make you free.

Jesus is the very personification of the life force of truth. He calls Himself truth in the book of John 14 vs. 6. Jesus personifies truth. He is the one who makes us free not truth in its mental sense as many think.

The word of God contains the life force of truth hidden in the scriptures. As you begin to romance the heart of God and grow in intimacy with Him through the word your spirit man slowly grows in glory. Notice what John says when he describes the glory they saw on Jesus.

John 1 vs. 14
"And the Word became flesh and dwelt among us, and we beheld His glory, the glory as of the only begotten of the Father, full of grace and *truth*".

See that? John says he could see the glory of God in Jesus. He could see the fullness of grace and truth on the Lord Jesus. How does one see truth on a person if truth was just a fact? Truth is a life force. It is living and the Lord Jesus Christ is the personification of it. You can see truth on him as a tangible substance.

The twofold effects of truth

Truth makes a way when there seems to be no way. It has a two-fold effect and Apostle Paul says it this way,

Hebrews 4:12
"For the word of God is quick, and powerful, and sharper than any two-edged sword, piercing even to the dividing asunder of soul and spirit, and of the joints and marrow, and is a discerner of the thoughts and intents of the heart".

Truth can either impart or destroy. It is sharp whichever way you look at it. Truth will pierce the lies of the devil. Truth has the ability to fight on our behalf. It is important to understand that truth will not tolerate lies. Truth will not tolerate anything that stands against it. It will destroy.

I heard about a man who when he spoke people would never believe a word that proceeded out of his mouth. I was told that if he were to tell you that it was morning you would have to double check on your own because he lied so much.

Seek truth through the personification of Christ. He is the truth and He is also the word. Learn the word and you have learnt truth. If you get to know Him and get intimate with Him, He reveals more and more of who He is to you. You begin to move in the realm of steadfastness, which is truth. You are not moved by anything or anyone. You are a force to be reckoned with.

There are people who cannot take a stand for truth. Their truth has no stability and is moved by any manner of doctrine. Today they are here and tomorrow they are there changing all the time like a chameleon. Take a look at what the bible says,

James 1 vs. 7-8
For let not that man suppose that he will receive anything from the Lord; he is a double-minded man, unstable in all his ways.

The word *double minded* is the word ***dipsuchos***, which actually means *double souled* from ***dis***, "twice," ***psuche***, "a soul."

A double-minded person is restless and confused in his thoughts, his actions and his behavior. Such a person is always in conflict with himself. One torn by such inner conflict can never lean with confidence of God and His gracious promises. This is the character of an outer court believer who is not yet well acquainted with his friend and lover.

Those who are double-minded do not have the faith spoken of in

Hebrews 11 vs. 1
"Now faith is being sure of what we hope for and certain of what we do not see.

A double minded person on the other hand is a faithless someone who cannot get himself to stick to one truth and never change.

And the things you do not want to do you do. Why, because the enemy has planted the seed of darkness in your life and only the truth will wipe that out.

The light of God is the truth of God. People do not relate truth in their thinking to the light of God coming from their life but it is related. Truth is tied up to glory. If you do not start changing your thought life now, the glory of God will be hindered and blocked in your own spirit, soul, and body. To see the glory of God shining forth from a person's life is the best thing possible on planet earth.

The bible tells us that one day the church of Jesus Christ will be so perfected that the world will look at the church and see the glory of God upon the covenant people of God. The glory of God, the truth of God affects our body by putting spiritual life and healing virtue into our body. We need to transform our heart and mind by learning, knowing, absorbing, dwelling in the truth of God. That is the power of God's transforming truth in the glory of God.

Knowing this Intimacy is what produces that aforementioned jittery kind of excited love you feel that makes you nervous in the right sense. It makes your palms sweat, your mouth goes dry, your heart races with excitement, butterflies in your stomach and even words stumble clumsily out of your mouth for the Lord. This is not sexual love like carnal people would want to think. This goes way beyond sexual love. It goes beyond the physical love that people get so caught up with. It is in its own grade and dimension. In this dimension true lovers stay close together and nothing else matters except their love for each other. It is a realm of only two!

Notice, true lovers are always together. They only see each other and only adore each other. Imagine that picture. Imagine it is you and the one you truly love. Just imagine that lover, never letting go and never letting loose. Imagine gazing into each other's eyes for eternity and realizing you never want it to end. Imagine that true lover as God.

That is exactly what God can be to you if you dare get the understanding of 'INTIMACY'. Dare to romance the heart of God!